THE WORLD RECORD BOOK OF RACIST STORIES

AMBER RUFFIN AND LACEY LAMAR

GRAND CENTRAL
PUBLISHING

New York Boston

Copyright © 2022 by Amber Ruffin and Lacey Lamar

Cover design by Albert Tang
Cover photo © Lloyd Bishop
Cover copyright © 2022 by Hachette Book Group, Inc.

Grand Central Publishing
Hachette Book Group
1290 Avenue of the Americas, New York, NY 10104
grandcentralpublishing.com
twitter.com/grandcentralpub

First edition: November 2022

Grand Central Publishing is a division of Hachette Book Group, Inc. The Grand Central Publishing name and logo is a trademark of Hachette Book Group, Inc.

The publisher is not responsible for websites (or their content) that are not owned by the publisher.

The Hachette Speakers Bureau provides a wide range of authors for speaking events. To find out more, go to www.hachettespeakersbureau.com or call (866) 376-6591.

Library of Congress Cataloging-in-Publication Data

Names: Ruffin, Amber, author. | Lamar, Lacey, author.
Title: The world record book of racist stories / Amber Ruffin and Lacey Lamar.
Description: First edition. | New York : Grand Central Publishing, 2022.
Identifiers: LCCN 2022026047 | ISBN 9781538724552 (hardcover) | ISBN 9781538724576 (ebook)
Subjects: LCSH: Racism—Humor. | United States—Race relations—Humor.
Classification: LCC PN6231.R25 R84 2022 | DDC 818/.602—dc23/eng/20220713
LC record available at https://lccn.loc.gov/2022026047

ISBNs: 9781538724552 (hardcover), 9781538724576 (ebook)

Printed in the United States of America

LSC-C

Printing 1, 2022

This book is dedicated to all white people everywhere... Just kidding! The opposite of that! This book is dedicated to our family and friends who experienced all these stories with us... Just kidding, this book is dedicated to El DeBarge!

Contents

One night, a few years ago, my white, male friend was late for a date with his wife. So, he was driving hastily and blew through a four-way stop sign. Immediately behind him he sees flashing lights. He's getting pulled over. He's in a car with very tinted windows in a Black neighborhood. He knew the police thought they were pulling over a Black person. The cop gets out of the car, and right away, unholsters his gun.

> Just a quick aside in the story—my friend is saying "unholstered his gun" in a way that leads me to believe that is not what he is used to when being approached by a cop. Fun!

My friend rolled his window down and stuck both hands out as the officer approached. When the officer gazed upon my friend's lily-white skin, he instantly holstered his gun. The cop asked politely why he had blown through the four-way stop sign. My friend told the officer he had just finished coaching soccer for a neighborhood school and one of the kids had left his book bag at the school and he was rushing to return it.

Just a quick reminder that this is a lie.

My bud gestured to the back seat where his own back-pack was. The officer asked for his license and registration. BOTH HAD EXPIRED.

Another quick aside to Black people to say, oh my god, you know that if your shit was expired you would not be going home that night. Except to your new home, JAIL FOREVER.

The officer says it will be just a minute and goes back to his car. My friend says he was gone maybe four minutes and returns and informs him that he really should take him in for the expired license and registration but instead, "I decided just to give you a ticket for both."

I am not kidding when I say, I did not know they could just give you a ticket for that. This book is educational. The person writing it is being educated. My word.

So, the officer gives him two tickets and sends him off on his merry way. He arrives at his dinner with his wife and all is well. After a short time, he receives a call. It's the damn OFFICER!!

> And this is where this story enters a realm of whiteness that I have only imagined.

The officer starts off APOLOGIZING for giving him a ticket in the first place. The cop says, "I can tell you were only trying to help your community, and I feel really bad for pulling you over. Hey, just rip up your ticket and I'll get rid of it on my end." Can you stand it?! Not to put too fine a point on it but, to this cop, giving a white guy tickets he deserves is considered too cruel.

Guys. I frigging love this story. Now, this isn't indicative of what you will find in this book, it's just the story that shocks me the most. I mean, I know, I know, I know, but daaang. Just thought we should take a look at the unbelievable before we dive in.

This is the *World Record Book of Racist Stories* brought to you by the Ruffins. The Ruffins are the cutest family you have ever seen in your dang life! Mom and Dad are from Georgia and Virginia and they moved to Omaha because they were stationed there when they were in the Air Force.

> I'm clearing that up because I don't want you to think these two Black adults looked at a map of

America and pointed to the dead center, and said, "There! This is the perfect place for our kids!" It was more of a "We've been living here for so long and now we are part of the community" type of thing.

So, this is the second book of racist stories our family has endured. For the first book, most of the stories centered around Lacey, and they were almost impossible to believe. Hence the title, *You'll Never Believe What Happened to Lacey*. But this book is gonna be a little different. Instead of just me and Lacey, there are stories about the whole family, all our siblings, and even some friends. We felt how great it was to air out our own dirty racist laundry and thought it would be cool to give other people the chance to do the same thing. And I think we are right!

Okay, so, we wrote this book for several reasons.

1. People honestly thought we didn't have more stories. So, it's kinda like a dare.
2. We like hanging out with each other.
3. It is good for you to write these stories down and let them go. It's pretty cool for a bunch of people to read them and shout into their books, "I know THAT'S right" or "I hate this! It can't be true!" But even just writing them out gives you a second to look at and process all this stuff.
4. We can't let one of us write down these stories alone.

That is true! Because Amber would write everyone's real first and last names, and we would get in trouble. I know you think she has common sense but she does not.

I honestly think I'm right on this one. I want everyone in this book to be put the fuck on blast! But I know that's not allowed, so we don't. So, if you feel like you recognize someone from one of these stories and their name is in this book, it is not them because I was forced to use a fake name!

Why are you acting like you have ever remembered a single person's name?

Because I remember everyone's name.

Okay. What's the name of my child?

Jarvis.

No.

Point taken. Can you believe there's enough stories for two whole books? I can! FYI: You'll be able to tell the difference between this book and the last book. This one's gonna be a bit heavier. A touch more serious. The reason for that is with the first book, Lacey and I got to giggle through silly racism stories, and it felt great. So, if the family wants to share their stories too, however they want to share, we welcome that. We want them to feel great and heard and blah, blah, bloo. There's plenty of silliness, it's just that the rest of the family is less likely to remember the funnier racist stories. They have not been keeping journals. But those terrible, scary racist stories? Maaaan, they remember those like a mug. So, to emotionally prepare you, I'd call this book fifty-fifty silly-scary racist stories. Okay? So, don't come to me talking about "It wasn't like the first book" 'cause you've been warned. It started with a white person story, for Pete's sake. It's gonna be a little different, okay?!

Soooo, what else do you need to know...My family is from Omaha, Nebraska, and Lacey still lives there. Racism is what you would expect in Omaha. There're more Black people than you think but also those racists are bold as hell! I live in New York City now, and I work in comedy, so I do not have nearly as many racist encounters as my family does. But I grew up in Omaha so I get it. And we think it's important to be able to say out loud (or write out loud) the racist things that have happened to you. It's okay to call racist things racist, and it's okay to be hurt by them. It's okay to laugh at them, it's okay to keep them to yourself, and luckily, it's okay to put all of 'em in a book and put some motherfuckers on blast! Just kidding. All the names have been changed unless they're our little friends.

Oh. And when you see Helvetica, it's Amber.

And when you see Bembo, it's Lacey!

As Lacey and I tell you our family's stories, please remember that she is old and gross, and I'm young and beautiful.

Okay, so just right out of the gate, you need to know that Amber is a fool.

A beautiful fool. Breathtaking, really. Okay. Lacey, please stop going on and on about my severe case of the cutes! Are we ready to start this book?

Yes! Yay!

THE WORLD RECORD BOOK
OF RACIST STORIES

CHAPTER ONE

SON OF A GUN!

approaches podium in a super-fancy ball gown

W elcome to the World Record Book of Racist Stories Awards! We are going to be awarding some prestigious titles tonight to people who have really earned them. Now, what is a racist? Is it just a confused person who means well but blah, blah, blah? No. A racist is a turd.

> Ooh! Quick sidenote: We will not be explaining shit in this book. So, if you want to know why we did what we did or if you want someone to explain what racism is, I cannot help you.

> Ooh! Side sidenote: Some of you, as you read this book, will want us to lament about how sad it is being in this cruel world, and you'll want to see some of that trauma porn-ish Black pain, but I'm

sorry to report, reading this book will leave you unsatisfied.

Our esteemed judges, Mommy, Daddy, Chrystal, Angie, Lacey, Jimmy, and Amber have searched their memories to bring you the best of the best. These racists we're honoring tonight have really applied themselves to their crafts. They've spent years preparing for these interactions. They're excellent at racism. As they would say about us, it's in their blood. First up, our award for:

LEAST "ALL BLACK PEOPLE LOOK ALIKE"

I was once pulled over while entering a ramp to the interstate. There was no reason for me to be pulled over. I had done everything right. I was going under the speed limit. My tags were good. We all know why I'm being pulled over. It was the middle of the day. So, I was immediately less scared than normal. The cop approaches the car. Now, we both know he's pulled me over for no reason. The trick here is sussing out whether he pulled me over because he's angry and racist or just racist. The way he started talking to me let me know he's pretty chill. As a result, I mustered up the courage to ask the officer why I was being pulled over. Now, that sounds like nothing, but the amount of courage it takes to ask an officer WHY you're being pulled over is the same amount it takes to fight a bear because that shit could have the same result. I knew there was no excuse and that he probably

2

wouldn't shoot me in broad daylight. So, I ask him and his reply is, "We are just doing some checks in the area."

What the hell is he checking on? Checking to see if my rights are still intact? THEY'RE NOT! Also, is this even a thing officers say?

Anyway, this guy asks me for my license and registration. I give him both. He immediately looks at my license and says, "This doesn't even look like you." I can't begin to explain to you how this picture looked EXACTLY like me. I know what you're thinking: *Your hair was different.* Nope! It was exactly the same. *The license was old.* Nope. I had just gotten the license a few weeks before the stop. I tell him, "Actually, I just got this license a few weeks ago, and it couldn't look more like me." He gives me a sarcastic laugh and "No it doesn't!" Now, some days you have common sense but this was not me on this day. Instead of being quiet and respectful I say back to him, "Yes it does." I don't know where I got the bravery from but as he walks away he yells back, "NO IT DOESN'T!" So I yell back even louder, "YES IT DOES!" After about ten minutes he comes back to my car and says all of my information checks out, and I can go. As he hands my license back to me he says, "This picture still doesn't look anything like you." I say back to him, "Yes it does, it looks just exactly like me." This is coming from a white police officer who works in a Black neighborhood, and he can't tell if a Black woman looks like the picture she presents to him? How can he be sure he's got the right suspect if he can't match a picture with a face?! What the hell will this man do if he accidentally stumbles upon a missing child? Carry around the milk carton with him to prove to her she's not the one who is missing? Poor hypothetical child.

The next day at work, I tell a white coworker that I was pulled over for no reason. He immediately tells me this just doesn't happen and there is always a reason. I tell him about the whole exchange, and he's shocked. This might be the first time he has heard a story like this from a person of color. He assures me that "doing some checks in the area" is not a thing. He looks at my license and all he says is "Wow, you may be right about that officer." My favorite thing to do was to show people the picture and ask them if they could believe he didn't think it looked like me. They can't. Also unbelievable: Our third-grade playground back-and-forth of "No, it doesn't!" "Yes, it does!" Ha, ha, ha! So lucky to be alive!

WORST MEMBER OF THE ASPCA

I was working at a retirement home and a white coworker was trying to talk to me about race during the morning meeting.

> Sidenote: Almost every morning meeting I have ever had is, at best, very bad. I cannot explain why this is the place for people's racism to come out. I'm not a scientist, but I assume it's because a lot of your racist coworkers wake up

> chock-full of racism and it has to come out early
> or else it puts their Black coworkers in danger of
> having a good day.

We have just had a very serious conversation about a resident who refuses to be helped by Black staff. This person does nothing but berate Black employees with racial slurs and sometimes physically tries to harm them. As I'm explaining how difficult it is to work with this resident and that several staff members are thinking about quitting because of him, my white coworker chimes in. I am not kidding you when I tell you this woman says, "I understand how hard it is being Black. Have you ever heard of the black dog campaign?"

Girrrrrrrllllll, so you know about being paralyzed with fear? Well, at this moment, I am paralyzed with racism. I know exactly what this woman's next words will be, and I know that they will be so racist that I'll remember them forever. Yet I am unable to stop the impending doom (or rather, impending dumb). I'm trying to figure out who in the world I can call to bail me out of jail. Who am I kidding? My bail will be set too high, and I will spend the rest of my life in prison. Deep breath. This woman says, "You know, black dogs never get adopted so it's very hard for them in the shelters because they are the first to be euthanized." Please. In the name of sweet Black baby Jesus explain to me what this has to do with this conversation? We are talking about human beings and this bitch is like "all dogs matter."

Anyways, after she says that, I fight her, and spend the rest of my life in jail. Just kidding. But I wish I had.

BEST EXAMPLE OF WHY WE NEED DIVERSITY TRAINING AT DIVERSITY TRAINING

This one is my favorite because I remember years ago when this happened and how hard I laughed. Lacey used to work with a man who was from a small town with absolutely no people of color, and it showed every time he opened his mouth. Let's call him Chris. When Lacey first met him, he would often ask her if she would get him a coffee from the break room. Like he was in charge of her. He was not. Lacey would always say the same thing, "No. I am never going to get you coffee because I am not your secretary. I'm no one's secretary. But if I were someone's secretary, it would not be for you because you do not have one." She had been at this company over ten years before he started working there and had never gotten anyone a cup of coffee. Chris would have to stay thirsty. For his first three months Chris constantly would ask Lacey about running track. Running track. Running. Lacey has not run since 1985. She does like to go to the gym, but she has always hated cardio. I mean hate it. She very does not run. If a bear was chasing her, she would lie down, sprinkle some salt on herself, and hand the bear a fork.

If I had to be bear dinner, I would want to be seasoned.

So no, she never ran track. He is shocked by this and *keeps asking her as if she forgot*! "Are you sure you never ran track? Come on, I bet you can run real fast." Once they were all walking back to the parking lot and Chris says, "Show me how fast you can run: let's race back to the cars. I know you must be fast, but I bet I can keep up."

Oh, I remember that day! We had just left the building getting ready to go home. So I said, "Sure, let's race." He was so excited as he yelled, "On your mark, get set, go!" He took off running like a bat out of hell never looking behind him, and I turned around and walked back in the building. He still didn't get the hint.

This is a thing some Black people have to endure when interacting with white people: they assume you are great at sports. Lacey asked him, "Why aren't you asking anyone else in the office if they ran track? I think you're assuming all Black people are good at sports. That's ignorant. You need to stop asking me this. It's making you look bad." So that's who we are dealing with here. THE STORY HASN'T EVEN STARTED!

Anyhoo, Lacey was at diversity training at work, and they were about to do a pretty common exercise. You know the one. Everyone is asked to stand in a line, and as certain life questions are asked you either step forward if you have benefited from your privilege or you take a step back if this affects you negatively due to race or socioeconomic background. As the exercise goes on most women and people of color are in the back of the room. But Chris is far ahead of everyone else when the exercise is over, meaning he is the most privileged. He yells out, "I won, I won! I won diversity training!" A human man yelled that for real. They all try to explain to him that this is not a game and that no one "wins" this exercise. This is to show how easy you have it in life and that you need to understand how white privilege works. Like a Will Ferrell character in a hilarious sketch, he talks over them the entire time, giddy as hell. He is too busy celebrating to listen. Then, and this is real, Chris goes into an acceptance speech about how his parents raised him right. And then, in a most unfortunate tangent, he blames people of color for not being respectful to police officers, saying this is why there are so many "problems" during police stops. This all took place AT diversity training. The trainer tried her best to explain it. He was not receptive. She never got through to him.

He continues to work there and nothing bad ever happened to him. In fact, there was a police investigation because there was a lot of money missing from the office. A lot of people thought Chris stole it, but there was no proof. Once the police got involved, Lacey just knew she was gonna get blamed because she's so very Black. But she didn't! Miracle! Chris, even though people thought he stole it, never got in trouble. He's probably working somewhere right now challenging his Black coworkers to races. And, in a way, because he got to arrive with racist beliefs, and leave with them *and* a job, he did. He did win diversity training.

MOST FRUGAL RACIST

For "Most Frugal Racist," it's a two-way tie between "Salmon" and "That's Thirty Dollars." Here's "Salmon."

Lacey's at one of her favorite fancy restaurants for her birthday. It's her and about fifteen Black women. At the end of their long table there is an old white couple sitting at a table for two. They've already started their meal. They are so close to Lacey and her friends that they have interjected themselves into their party and most of their conversation. This is a dumb thing to do.

I know that we should have put an early stop to that but they were so fun and nice! You would have done the same thing!

You may have a point. I do like it when old people are fun. So, they all laugh and have fun together until the old couple gets their doggy bag. The food is wrapped in foil like a swan. At Lacey's table, some of the people in her party were still waiting for their meal.

Our lawyers have reviewed this book and they ask that at this point, you reach out and grab on to the most stable thing near you.

This couple, you guys, this old weird ass white couple stood up and walked to the head of Lacey's table to make a speech. They told them that they barely touched their extremely expensive salmon. They then did something un-believable. They offered Lacey and her friends their leftovers. Now, that is already the worst thing on planet Earth but it gets even worse! They went on to say if Lacey and her friends didn't feel like paying full price for a meal and wanted to save money they could BUY their barely touched salmon for a good price. BUY IT. Upon their saying this, Lacey's spirit was knocked into another galaxy where it is socially acceptable to cuss out old people in public and she said, "You ancient raggedy fucks, how dare you try to sell us food you have touched. The level of clean you would have to be for me to take a bite of your food after you've eaten it does not exist. If you couldn't afford to take your salmon home and reheat it later tonight, then maybe you can't afford to eat here, bitch. I know we had a fun fifteen minutes sitting together, but now, I have to beat your asses."

Okay that didn't really happen but in my heart it did.

Then, her spirit returned to this realm where the entire table of her friends was laughing as the couple walked away because it was the looniest thing they had ever heard. Eating food strangers have touched?! There is no way that if they had been a table full of old white men he would have tried to sell them his discounted salmon. If this has ever happened to any old white men, please contact Lacey.

I'm serious. Please let me know the restaurant, meal, and price tag. I'm very curious.

Just for fun, here's a list of people I will not share my food with for fear of catching their disgusting germs:

Mom
Dad
Chrystal
Angie
Jimmy
Amber
Jesus
My own dang child

And here's "That's Thirty Dollars."

One day I visited the Omaha Zoo with some friends. We decided to meet for lunch first. During lunch my girlfriend was telling me how one of her favorite parts of my book was how people always tell me how expensive things are when I ask for prices. Everyone at lunch could totally relate and we all had a good laugh sharing our "this is really expensive" stories. We arrive at the zoo and have a great time walking around, enjoying the animals and the great weather. When leaving the zoo, we decide to walk through the gift shop. I told my girlfriends that my daughter was just here, and I wanted to show them the big stuffed animal she just bought. I pull the huge stuffed stingray off the shelf and all of a sudden a small white child comes flying out of nowhere and yells, and I mean yells, "That's thirty dollars!" I look right at him. He is holding a small toy, and his mom is standing behind him with her hands crossed and nodding her head yes, as if to say, *Yes this is very expensive.* He tells me he looked at the stingray but his mother is making him get the smaller, cheaper toy. I replied, "Yes! I can see that it's thirty dollars because they put the price right here. My daughter just bought the stingray, but your toy is very nice." I added that my daughter bought the stingray just so the mother would know yes, we can afford this. My friends say he was standing there, just staring so hard, waiting for me to put it back. I say I know, he really wanted me to put it back on the shelf. But I did not. I can't explain the disapproval on the mother's face of me holding that "beyond expensive" stingray. How angry she was watching me walk around the store with it still in my arms when she left. Wondering if I would purchase this stupid toy and start a stingray collection. Her son is very good at price-checking people, got to start them early.

CHAPTER TWO

WHAT'S WRONG WITH YOU?

I've learned that people will forget what you said, people will forget what you did, but people will never forget how you made them feel.

—Maya Angelou

I will never forget the fact that this fool said this right to my beautiful face.

—Lacey Lamar

MOST CONFUSING RACIST PHRASE

Once in an office job, I worked with a bitter, old, Southern white woman. She kept her distance, and I kept mine. We both liked it this way. But, over time, unfortunately she warmed up to me. Believe me when I say you do not want a mean, old, Southern white woman to try to befriend you. I know, that's not nice, but it is also not a lie. Once she saw I was good at my job and not like all the "bad Black people" she sees on her TV, she gave me the dreaded "Lacey, I like you, you're not like other Black people" speech that some Black people get bestowed upon them like it's a wonderful compliment. All that speech does is let me know you have come to a bunk conclusion about Black people and you likely believe a bunch of other lies. It's a good warning to never start a conversation with you about the shape of the earth.

I avoided her like the plague because I never knew what old-timey, racist Southern craziness was going to spew out of her mouth. Her being an old, bitter white lady in Omaha is enough of a red flag, but you add on "Southern" and you just know you're in for some shit. And, in for it I was! You know how when you're working, you hum songs to yourself? Maybe it's a Top 40 hit, maybe it's old nineties music. Well, this woman would sing such greatest hits as "Jimmy Crack Corn" and "Camptown Races." Now, I'm aware that many parts of this book seem made up, like this one, but they're not. Here this old white woman is, congratulating me on not being a Black stereotype when she is a stereotypical daughter of the Confederacy. Do you know how many verses there are in "Camptown Races"? A lot, and she knew every last one. She had to be pulled aside and told that these songs were not appropriate for work and were actually racist. Maybe I listened in to her being reprimanded and maybe I didn't. (I did.) She was like, "What?! I've sang these songs since I was a child!" She said that like children can't be racist! Now, I did not know her when she was a child but Imma go ahead and say she was theeee racist of the playground. I mean, we all know you sang scary songs but it's not going to fly here, not with all these free Black people working around you.

Anyway, one day I heard her looking for something at her desk. She is muttering over and over, "Where is it?! Where the hell is my calculator?!" She became more and more agitated. "I know someone stole it, some people you just can't trust." Now, I know exactly where this is going 'cause I know which coworkers she perceives to be untrustworthy. I think, *She's going to go up to all the Black employees and accuse them of theft.* Boy, am I wrong. This woman reaches peak frustration, and then it came out of her mouth. She said it, you guys. She yelled the most confusing and racist phrase I've ever heard. She yells, "I'll tell you, there's a nigger in the haystack somewhere!" Yep. That's what she said. Let's break that phrase down even though it will do us no good:

Okay, so this seems to come from the phrase "Like looking for a needle in a haystack," which means "hard to find." So, if we take out "needle" and put in a whole person, then it becomes pretty easy to find. I feel like if I was hiding in a haystack, you'd only need a minute or so to get to me. So, that makes the whole phrase fall apart. Does it mean "In every haystack, there's always an n-word"? 'Cause again, that is nonsense, the amount of hay that would get stuck in our hair alone! I feel confident in saying that you will never find a Black person in any haystack. We would never be in a haystack. Too itchy. And, if this phrase was supposed to mean, "Behind every stolen thing, there's a guilty Black person," well, that's just not the correct way to say that. And, of course I have a problem with you insinuating that, but it's such a muddy way to communicate such an easy-to-grasp idea. 2 out of 10—almost intelligible.

Okay. You guys are not gonna believe this. Lacey told me the history of this phrase and it's outstanding. After she told me this story, the phrase was really bothering her. She tried googling it (I try not to google bad things so my internet experience stays toxic in a more targeted way), and she found the origin of that phrase!!! It comes from a cartoon that is a racist parody of Abraham Lincoln trying to downplay his abolitionist stance to voters. It's a cartoon drawing of him on a woodpile with a Black person in it. There's a Democrat saying, "Hey! There's an n-word in the woodpile." So as to say, you're trying to get away with giving Black people rights! So, it grew to mean something is suspicious or wrong. And then kind of merged with "needle in a haystack" because of stupidity. Are you guys ready to see the cartoon? Here you go!

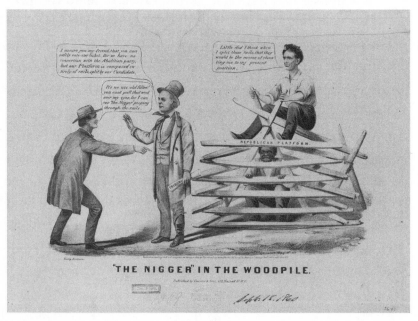

This isn't about that cartoon, but damn. So, where were we? The woman had just dropped an n-bomb so loud, it stunned the entire office. At that point I look over at her, right in her face, and she looks right back at me and continues to hunt for her calculator, leading me to believe this woman actually thinks you can say this at work. Which makes me wonder where in the world did she work before this?

Had to be any other place in Omaha, Nebraska.

Shut up, Amber. Quit telling the truth. Also, I had never in my life heard this phrase and have never heard it since. I truly thought I had heard every racial slur in the world. But it just goes to show you, you really do learn something new every day! Luckily, there was a Black supervisor in earshot who swept her away and gave her the lecture of her life on how that is not appropriate and told her she would have to be written up. Maybe I listened in and maybe I didn't. (I did.) This is a very rare moment where I actually saw someone reprimanded for racist behavior. When she comes back to her desk she can't stop telling me how she absolutely did not use the n-word in a racist way. I let her know there is no other way she could have used it.

This incident doesn't get her fired. The incident that does, though, is pretty great. This woman ends up working for the company a few months longer until she is fired for embezzling thousands of dollars. Yay!

Since the first book was written I've had several white people come up to me and basically ask, "If all those things are racist, then, what *can* we say? It seems like a large amount of what white people said to you in your book was offensive." To them I say, VERY PERCEPTIVE. Just kidding. I never answer that question, but I think maybe I should. Now, I can't speak for every Black person in the world, but I can tell you what has been said to me that I never want to hear again. Here's a list of actual things that were said AFTER the first book was written. I think you're gonna like it. Just kidding.

1. "Why is your hair like that? That's an old lady hairstyle and it looks terrible." You will read about this later in the book, but it's so hilarious I had to mention it twice!

2. Lacey's waiter can't stop recommending that she order the fried chicken, and he nearly fainted when she told him she almost never eats it. He said, "That's so weird, because most—" Then she tells him, "Please don't, I really want to eat here, just take my order."

3. "Lacey, for our bank meeting, please make sure you wear something nice and your nails and hair are done. It's important to look put together." Wow, have you ever seen me look any other way?

4. "Jews are really stingy; you have to be careful working with them." This is also something white people do. Start talking to you about other cultures because as long as it's not about you they are

not being racist. YES, YOU ARE. We will touch on this later.

5. "Did you know that Jews are not regular white people? They actually look different."

6. "My husband just wants to touch your hair."

7. I'm at a brunch and a white woman asks me if Amber's hair is a wig. What? Why? Oh okay, let me get her on the phone, she loves to have conversations with strangers about her hair!

8. I was recently told by a white man during a business meeting that "Yes, a lot of white musicians stole Black music, but did you know Michael Jackson stole the hook from 'Under Pressure'? So, see Black people steal music from whites, too!" First, what the hell are you talking about? And second, this is not a record company. Why are we talking about this? Is this one of those moments where you heard one Black person on TV say something and it rubbed you the wrong way and now you're using me to try and make your point no one cares about? Guys, no Black person represents all Black people. Except me right now for this one second as I say to that guy, "You are an idiot for bringing this up."

9. "If establishments are in Black neighborhoods they don't do well, they need to be in more diverse areas so that EVERYONE is comfortable." Okay so, one million things are wrong with that statement. If being the only white person somewhere makes

you uncomfortable, too frigging bad. And exactly how are you using the word "diverse"? Also, I feel like what you're saying is there should be no businesses in Black neighborhoods because white people are too scared to go there? Please just say what you mean. I have been approached to back business ideas in Omaha and have been told this before. Let me be clear: don't bring that ignorance around me.

10. Because nine is uneven!

MOST ANGRY ABOUT MY HAIR

I need everyone to know it is a running joke in my family that I have horrible luck when I go to get a manicure. The salon stories alone could be their own book.

Guys. She is not kidding. But what she's not telling you is it's the same place she keeps going back to. Every time I go there, I have a blast and they are so nice, and every time Lacey goes there, something hilarious happens. Baseline is the nails look bad. But once, Lacey, her daughter, Imani, and I went together and got our nails done and Lacey's lady told her an extremely sad and long and personal story that Lacey never asked to hear. And, every time she talked, she stopped working. So, she never finished Lacey's nails. Lacey just had to leave with undone nails. We teased her for a week. One lady took her and angrily did her nails the whole time, referring to the white woman Lacey was "forcing to wait for her" by getting her nails done. As if Lacey told her to stop doing that woman's nails and start on hers.

Recently, I went to get a manicure at that same place I shouldn't be going to. I get in and the receptionist is the owner and she is meaner than mean. But you know she's in charge and it makes you feel taken care of. So, she angrily sends me to a manicurist and while the manicurist is doing my nails she won't stop looking at my hair. She is just staring at it. Mind you, she should be looking at my nails, but will not stop looking at my head. She says, "Your hairstyle is something that old ladies wear. It's big and frizzy, it's just so old looking, like it's something my mother would wear." Even though you already know this, I'm wearing an Afro. I tell her, "Well, actually a lot of people tell me that they like my hair and it looks nice." She just keeps talking right over me and says it just looks so old like something from the sixties and seventies. I tell her "Well, you would be right about that. Afros were very popular then, and they are popular now." That doesn't stop this woman. I think her goal is to make me agree with her? I do not know why she is doing this. It's baffling to me. Usually, I can tell you where the behavior is coming from, but this is something new. She continues, "It just looks terrible! I mean it's either this or an old lady bun." I don't know what she means by that but she repeats it again. "This"—she points to my hair, like I don't know what she's talking about—"or an old lady bun." I try to stop the conversation by saying, "Can you just finish my nails? I have an appointment I need to get to." She finally stops talking to me about it, and when she is done I walk up to the cash register to pay. The owner, who knows me and I swear could hear the whole conversation, asks me how everything was. Now, as mean as the owner is, I know she did not come to play. I tell her, "Horrible. She kept telling me how awful my hair looked and told me it looked like an old lady hairstyle." The only upside to that experience was that I got a free manicure.

It's actually a downside. This place is the worst, and Lacey went back to it to get yet another bad manicure.

Ooh! Sidenote: The title of this book was almost *"Your Hair Is Old and Terrible" More Racist Stories*.

LET'S GET SIDETRACKED FOR A SECOND

So, there is this fascination with Black people's hair in and outside of work that truly baffles me. I know a lot of white people are curious about our hair, and let me be clear: you are owed nothing, and we don't enjoy being interrogated. It is not our job to educate you. When you ask, "Is this your real hair?" It's like, okay, why does this matter to you? What could you possibly gain from knowing this? Why would you ask someone if something on their body was real? Listen to yourself. Can I come in and ask, "Hey Fred, are those your real teeth?" "Hey Janice, are those your real boobs?" Imagine in the middle of a meeting I turn to Sarah and ask aloud, "You a bottle blonde or a real blonde?" It's the same damn thing.

Also, every time someone says, "Your hair is so cool! I wish my hair looked like that." You wish you had an Afro? Sixty-two-year-old Norwegian Diane from HR wished she had natural Black hair? First off—no you don't, you're lying. You wouldn't last a day with this hair; you wouldn't know where to begin. Michael Jackson had Black hair his whole life and he almost burned to death. The prep work and products alone would have your head spinning. Do you have seven hours to spend on your day off at the natural hair salon that is impossible to get into to have your hair done? 'Cause you're going to need help, Diane. A lot of help. And let's just be honest; you would look like a fool. A culturally appropriating fool. Here is a pic of Diane in an Afro.

See? Less fun than you thought. My point is, the white person should be made to wear the Black hairstyle they say they want so badly for a day. They would shut the hell up. Now, the next thing people do is ask, "How did you do it?" Now, do you think I want to give a natural hair tutorial in the middle of the morning meeting? Actually, that sounds like fun. I would love to give a tutorial. But not at my job! If you are so curious, google it. And do you really want a play-by-play on how my hair was cornrowed? You don't! Now, this is a real question and I've been asked this many times: "Do you wash your hair?" Why are you asking me this? You're asking me if I have washed a part of my body while I'm sitting in a room full of people. You're asking, at this moment, if my hair is dirty? Do you know how demeaning you sound? Do you wash your ass? I hope the answer is yes. Now let's revisit another subject, because since the first book came out it is still happening, and I truly don't think it will ever stop. Please for the love of Pete, don't touch my hair. It's sad to say but it still happens. Can I touch a part of your body? Just any old part? You'd probably say no. This is how we feel. If we have not given you permission just assume you can't run up and touch someone's hair. Now, I know some of you might be asking, "Wow, what can I say?" Great question! You can just say, "I like your hair. It looks nice." Compliments are always good when they aren't rude, ignorant, or intrusive. Or you can even say nothing. Ahhh, walking into work and actually just working without the focus being on my hair would be great.

And if you feel like, "Yeah. This is well-worn territory," guess how the hell I feel? I am not exaggerating when I say it takes up so much of my time. I can't tell you how the beginning of countless days at work have been focused on my hair. Let me paint the picture:

You have changed your hairstyle. It cost six hours and minimum $150. You know you look great. You go to work and as you get out of the car, the realization sets in—this will be the topic of conversation for the entire day. You make the dreaded walk from the parking lot to the door, knowing the dumbass questions are about to flow. You do a few stretches before you open the door so you can stay limber enough to swat the inevitable white hands from your hair. But, it's okay. You're one of a million Black people at work. Just kidding! You're a speck of pepper in a bowl of grits! You sit in the morning meeting and the questions and comments begin:

What the hell did you do?
Are those boxed braids?
This is like the movie *B.A.P.S!*
How much did this cost? Can you afford it?
Got a new wig, huh?
So, what is this? Yarn?
I liked your hair better the other way.
I hated your hair the other way.
Do we have a new employee?
So, do you sew this directly to your scalp? Or . . . ?
Can I touch it?
Did you use glue?

You really need to consider straightening it so you can look normal.

Will you take it off and let me wear it?

Do you know my friend, Lacey Lamar?

When I am faced with all of these terrible comments, I think: What can I do to help people with their compulsive commenting on Black people's hair? And, I think I found the answer. The Hands-Outta-Your-Hair Oath. I'm going to need the white people reading this right now to raise their right hand and repeat after me:

I, [my full white name], promise to never ask these questions or make these comments to Black people no matter how well I think I know them. I will keep my hands to myself. Unless I want to save Amber from a dragonfly caught in her Afro like there was years ago at a McDonald's and people watched in horror as she cried, flopping around looking like she was fighting a ghost. Then and only then are my hands allowed in someone's hair. Whether I think it looks good, whether I think it looks bad, when my Black friend or coworker shows up with a new do I will look them dead in the eye and say "You look great!" or I will shut the fuck up.

Great job! By taking that pledge, you've earned your very own Certificate of Black Hair Allyship! Sign the next page and rip it out! Frame it and put it on your wall! And, this part is important, when your Black friends come over, don't point it out to them!

WORST-TIMED RACISM

Later on that same day as the "Angry about my hair Incident" I went on a first date at a restaurant. My date wanted to sit at the bar, which should have been my first clue it wasn't going to work out but that's not what this story is about.

Read about all of Lacey's dates in her next book called, *Lacey, the Bad Date Magnet.*

Shut up, Amber. So, we sit at the bar and as our food arrived one of the bartenders comes over and says, "See that old man at the other end of the bar? Whatever you do, do not make eye contact with him." I start to laugh, and he says, "I'm not joking, he basically lives here and just annoys everyone he talks to." For fun, let's call this guy Old Talky. I thank the bartender for the tip because I definitely don't want to spend any time talking to— And before I can finish, Old Talky is making his way over to us. We are the only Black people at the bar, and I can see exactly where this is going. This man sits right down next to us and says, "Hey, where are you guys from?" We both say we are from Omaha, and his eyes light up. He starts talking about how he is a plumber, and he has helped a lot of poor Black people in Omaha with their plumbing. Just in case you thought you read that wrong he started the conversation by saying he has helped a lot of poor Black people. Now, this is not the first nor last conversation I have had like this. People come in hard and crazy with stories like this in hopes you will say, "Oh my god, thank you so much for saving us. You are a great person!" And, just in case anyone like that is reading this now, STOP TRYING TO GET BLACK PEOPLE TO THANK YOU ON BEHALF OF OTHER BLACK PEOPLE. THANK-YOUS DON'T WORK LIKE THAT. Anyway, this idiot's eyes light up with true love for his philanthropic self as he says, "I've helped so many Black single moms. You know, you go into those homes and you do the work and then when you tell them how much it's going to be, say it's like two hundred dollars, and you see them pull out a wad of money. And you notice it's fives and ones? I just tell them to stop. The work is free. Because you know they don't have enough money to pay you."

Hey, did you guys forget I was on a first date? Well, I didn't! I don't even respond to his dumbass story. Instead, I say, "Hello, we are on a first date." This fool smiles and KEEPS TALKING. He does not say, "Oh wow, don't want to bother you two, let me leave." Nope. He just keeps talking. But he's getting nothing in return. He then starts naming Black people he knows in Omaha to keep the conversation going. I don't have to tell you that there is no Black person he could name who would get me. I don't care if you know every Black person I do. If this man had said, "Do you know Lacey Lamar?" I would have been like, "I have no clue who you are talking about." I keep waiting for my date to save us, but if he had, this story wouldn't be in the book. Also, my date is splitting his attention between sports on the TV behind the bar and sports on the TV behind the bar.

Old Talky stays with us for an hour and a half. The whole damn date. He doesn't leave. I know it seems impossible to let this go on for so long but this is where my Midwestern sensibilities come into play. Calling him out would have led me to really losing my mind, my date would have seen that, and then I'd have been embarrassed. At least I had food. One of the many stories he divulged was how he told his church about "us." He actually said those words to me. "I told my church about you guys. How much I help Black people and about how you pay in fives and ones and they cried. They actually cried!" At this point, I tell him, "You know, I wrote a book about white people coming up to me and telling me stories just like this. Please read it." And then Old Talky takes out a small piece of paper from his pocket and writes down the name of my book. I told him it's about all my ignorant, racist encounters. And he still doesn't get that I'm talking about him, too. If anyone knows Old Talky the white plumber who helps poor Black people in Omaha, ask him what he thought of my book. He'll probably say he helped me write it.

Anyway, right at that time I see my friend Morgan and her husband! I motion for them to come over to us. Thank the Lord. So, I say to Old Talky, "Oh! My friends are here, and you're sitting in their spot." I quickly tell my friends they have to sit down. Mind you, Old Talky is still talking to my date, and if he had stopped talking about helping poor Black people long enough, my date would have heard me say, "Please save me from this ignorant white man!" They immediately see the pain on my face and sit down while he moves out of the way. I tell them all of the crazy mess he had been saying to us. He goes back over to the end of the bar and pays his tab, puts on his coat, and gathers his things, and I'm thinking, *Wow. I'm finally free and I never have to listen to this man again.* As I'm talking to my friends he comes back over to us on his way out. But this time, he squeezes in and stands close to me. This fool asks me, "Who are your people?" I feel like I'm about to lose my mind. Now I'd be double embarrassed for giving Old Talky the execution he deserves because there are now two extra witnesses. I politely say, "I don't think you know my family." Old Talky says, "What's your mom's name?" This man has assumed my mom is a single mom because she is a Black mom. I say, "BOTH my parents are Ruffin." Then, he says, "Maybe I've helped your mom, what is her name?" Still not clocking that some Black people have married parents. I tell him again, "You never helped my mother, and my parents are married. Always have been." Old Talky gives my elbow a squeeze, heads for the door, and turns back for a final, "I've helped so many single moms" and then walks out.

If you ever see me run screaming from a bar, it is because I saw him there. Pay me no mind.

WORST BIRTHDAY

I was working at a bank, and it was regular Omaha bad. But I had a fine working relationship with the other employees. Not like a "text you when something's funny" relationship but like an "ask you how your weekend was and not really mean it" relationship. It was your regular, run-of-the-mill "try to touch your hair" crowd. It did have a few "Black talking for fun" type of people who'd ask you like "What's crackalackin'?" and call you "girrrrlllll." When I worked there, I packed a lunch and always included a pack of Ho Hos. These sweet treats saved many a life. They kept me calm and full of sugar when I could've easily verbally executed these people for a number of reasons. These treats were my rock. On my birthday, I arrived at work and saw there were Ho Hos everywhere. They were hanging from the ceiling with paper clips. They were taped around my desk. I mean, they were everywhere. My white coworkers gathered around and shouted "Happy birthday!" And, for one split second, I actually thought, *Wow. An actual thoughtful thing from otherwise crappy people. Maybe I'm wrong. Maybe they are just reaching out in their own special way and I would have to try to evolve to be able to see the good in*— Just then, I look up and above my workspace these people had hung a large sign that said "Ho Ho Queen." Some of you reading this will see the problem with that right away; others will need a more in-depth explanation that they will never receive. Just kidding. When speaking to or about a Black woman please avoid anything that has the word "ho" in it. Even if it is a delicious chocolaty treat sent from the gods. There was no mistake in their little joke. They all took turns saying, "You're the *Ho* Ho queen!" I think they thought I thought it was funny. I think they thought it would actually be a good idea to call the only Black woman at their job a *ho*[*] all day long on her birthday. Y'all, the way they kept saying, "Hey *Ho* . . . Ho queen" and snickering was going to get me sent straight to prison. I immediately got up on my desk and took the sign down. I let them know there was no way in hell that any of this is appropriate. They disagree and say I'm being too sensitive. We are about to open up for business and I have no choice but to leave all the Ho Hos hanging from the ceiling. I'm pissed. Several Ho Hos are dangling above my head, so as customers are coming in naturally, they are asking about

---

[*] I know in the last book we all agreed the best way to spell this was "heaux" but I decided to go with "ho" because of the snack cake. Please forgive me.

them. My coworkers would tell them about my birthday and laugh. And as bad as it was, most of the customers would just look at my coworkers and feel embarrassed for me, because they realized I did not think it was funny. After about an hour or so of their joke not getting the response they wanted they ended up taking them Ho Hos down. I also wanted to take them heaux down. But I didn't. No one got punched, and I deserve a medal.

BEST USE OF CHILDREN

When Lacey's daughter, Imani, was in elementary school, Lacey picked her up for a doctor's appointment. She walks into the classroom to pop her head in really quick, snatch her child and go, when she sees a little Black girl massaging the shoulders of the twenty-something white lady teacher. (I realize this book is asking a lot of you, but could you do me a favor and for just a moment imagine such a thing? Honestly, my mind can't even conjure up such a picture. This young white woman is getting rubbed up by a small Black girl. Good lord. It's awful.) Lacey doesn't see her child in the room. The teacher doesn't register Lacey's disgust. "Where is my child?" she asks. "In the next classroom." Lacey walks next door and guess what, chicken butt? In the next classroom there's a Black child giving *that* young white lady teacher a massage. And, to make sure you understand the horror, it's this: The teacher is leaning all the way back in her chair with her head dangling over the edge. The little kid has his hands in her *hair*, massaging her scalp. The teacher is groaning in satisfaction. Sweet baby Jesus. The teacher sees Lacey and jerks upright. Unlike the first teacher, she knows this behavior is insane. So, Lacey gives the teacher a look and in a chipper voice, says to Imani, "Get your things, sweetie, and meet me out front!" She goes to the principal's office. They're not there. She says to the receptionist, "I need to talk to someone today about what I just saw." They give her a phone number to call. Imani walks up. "Let's go see the doctor!" On the way to the doctor Lacey ever so delicately asks Imani what in the world that was. She doesn't want to alarm her and has to be gentle to get the whole story. The whole story is this: At the end of the day, the good kids get to give the teachers back rubs. I would like to remind you that this is real life. Soooooooo, these women were grooming these children to be easy targets for pedophiles. "Rubbing my adult body is normal. Your reward is you get to touch me." Y'all. Now, were these two women pedophiles? Probably not. But are these children getting groomed none-theless? Yes.

Lacey calls the head of Omaha Public Schools, and he is disgusted. This man is livid. Thank god these teachers were white, or they'd have probably gotten fired. So, a few days later, Imani comes home with a letter explaining what happened and how the school will do better in the future. Frustrated, Imani said, "Some parent complained and now we can't give the teachers back rubs anymore!" This child had no clue.

Imagine if it was a little white boy and he had his fingers in my dreads. Scandal! Only white people would be like,

"Let me make this child physically give me pleasure." They'd be so sad. A white child's hands in my dreads! People would die! Wait. Imagine a Black *man* and a little white girl. Within minutes, you'd be able to find him—Up. Under. The. Jail. We still refer to this place as the School of Massage Therapy.

CHAPTER THREE

MOMMY AND DADDY STORIES

O ur next category is one of the larger ones. We have been taking a look at our present-day stories, which are of course, outstanding. But what happens if we find two Black adults and ask them for their superlatives? This next category, that's what. Our mom and dad have a rich history with racism. It was strong as hell when they were born and now, well, it's still doing pretty great. Our parents have lived a thousand lives at this point and have had about a million racist interactions, so it's important to remember why we chose these particular stories to be nominated. It's because they were the ones Mom and Dad remembered at the time I sat down with them, Lacey, and the computer. It's also important to remember that their stories will be different from mine and Lacey's. These stories will take place in a time when racist incidents were even more likely to end in jail time or damage to personal property or worse. They had to deal with some things I've only seen on TV. They're strong and smart and have been through a lot, and here's a little bit of it. Also remember these two lovebirds are living their best life with a huge family. They're fine. Wait, they're more than fine because they have a perfect child.

It's me. I'm their perfect child.

She is not. Here are their nominees.

WORST REACTION TO A NICE CAR

It's 1968 and a man named George Wallace is running for president. He's an Alabama governor who loves segregation and has locked in the racist vote. His name is wielded like Trump's at that time. Saying you're gonna vote for him is a fun, low-key way to tell your buds that you heart white supremacy. In 1968, Mom worked for Peter Kiewit, one of the largest construction companies in the world. It was her job to find inconsistencies in the spending for each project. This meant she was above a lot of white people. Which also meant that these people hated her guts. Now, this was back in the day, so it wasn't like the hate one might experience today. It was more of a "Black people are gross" type of hate that goes all the way back to "They're my property." Sooooo that's the vibe. Welp, when Mom gets this job, she had just purchased a brand-new '68 Mercury Cougar. In 1968. It was gold and black and Mom's true favorite child. This story is not about how cool a car this was but, just for fun, let's all take a look at it.

And then add to that how cute Mommy is:

So, let's put them together:

Then, maybe you can understand how mad these people were with her. Okay, so one day at this horrible job, Mom was in the office with two white coworkers. Another white coworker marches in talking about *her* new 1968 black and gold Mercury Cougar and how it's a shame there are two of them. She says very loudly to the whole group while making eye contact with Mom, that she's gonna have to get a George Wallace sticker to differentiate the two cars from each other.

Now, I have a lot of experience with racist stories but Mommy and Daddy? They are connoisseurs. This story receives high marks for subtlety but low marks for cowardice. 5/10.

MOST RACIST POTTY BEHAVIOR

Also at Peter Kiewit, the women's restrooms had three stalls, which was not enough for the amount of women working on Mom's floor. There was always a line, yet whenever Mom would come out of a stall, no one would use it. They would just wait until a white person had come out of a stall and use that one.

This story receives high marks for fucked-up-edness but again, cowardly. 7/10.

MOST RACIST BUS DRIVER

Dad joined the Air Force out of high school. So, when he was nineteen, he was coming home from basic training. Between basic training and your permanent assignment, they buy you a ticket home for a few weeks to visit your family. At Lackland Air Force Base in Texas, Dad boarded the Greyhound bus. But instead of an express bus, he got on one that hit EVERY LITTLE SOUTHERN TOWN between Texas and Portsmouth, Virginia. Along the way, the bus stops in a small town in Alabama. Dad got off and went to the restroom. As Dad was standing at the urinal, a big white man—the bus driver—came in and stood at the urinal next to him and said, "I ought to kick your ass." Dad was stunned. Usually when white people decide to get mad at you, they make up a reason. But this was out of nowhere. Confused, Dad smiled and shrugs. He finishes peeing and leaves. Once outside, he saw the "Whites Only" sign. That's when he realized what the bus driver was saying.

And I made this pretty clear in the first book, but I just want to reiterate how chill my frigging dad is. Every year we used to have a big cookout for the Fourth of July. At that cookout we would play volleyball—boys versus girls. And every year the girls won. We did this by...ummm, how should I say?...implementing our own set of rules. For instance, if you were really cute, you could have a do-over; if the ball didn't make it over the net, that was the net's fault. And we had regular boundaries on our side, but the boys' side of the court had no out-of-bounds. If it made it over the net and they didn't hit it, that's a point for us. Stuff like that. Now, if you're a friend of ours or a neighbor or a normal person, this makes you angry, but all of this is allowed because Dad is all like, "Let them have the ball. They're fine." We all had the time of our lives playing those games. This man is so committed to the happiness of his daughters that he let us win every year for our whole lives. And we win graciously. Just kidding. Every year, we gave everyone on the boys' team a woman's name (so they would be worthy of playing us) and sang special songs about winning. Oh my god, I'm remembering all this as I'm writing it down. The song goes like this:

♪♪How does it feel to lose?
Doesn't it feel like you?♪♪

Also, one time, many years ago, my brother's phone rang an odd musical ring no one had ever heard before. We joked

41

about how it sounded like an R&B love song. By the second ring, we had written a song that we would sing to the boys every volleyball game and still sing to Jimmy till this day:

♪♪Boy you know that you're the one
You're the only one for me
You know you make my life complete
And I'm never gonna let you go♪♪

Here is a list of some of the guys' volleyball names.

Blanche
Shoshona
Ester
Juliana

And Dad's volleyball name was Ballerina Girl.

And this is the picture that earned him that name. Doesn't he look like a beautiful ballerina girl? More graceful than we could ever hope to be.

MOST RACIST WORK SCHEDULE

So, Mom was in the Air Force, too. Mom and Dad were stationed at Offutt Air Force Base. (Once you get on it, you never get Offutt! No, that doesn't make a lot of sense but people love to say that.) At this time, there weren't many Black women in the Air Force. The women's barracks always had to have a woman whose duty it was to keep watch. Like a receptionist. And this duty was split between the women, white and Black. Independent of barracks duty, they all had weekends off. So, in order to keep the white women's weekends free, they rigged the schedule. Black women never had a day off because they had to work on Friday night because there's no work on Saturday and on Saturday night because there's no work on Sunday. But the white women were freeeeeee the whole weekend.

I think this story deserves a 3/10 because you just KNOW it was these same racists getting drunk all weekend at the local hangout spots. This racism probably saved a lot of Black people from going to those same bars and having a bad time.

FUNNEST FIGHT

Dad says he's always noticed that most of the time when white people pick on Black people, they'd always pick on those who were smaller or unintimidating. Hence the first book of all the stuff people said to Lacey! So, oftentimes they'd wind up picking on the smallest person and after a while that can break you down. Mom and Dad are pretty small. I'm the big one in the family and I'm five foot six. So, this resulted in Dad getting picked on a lot. He would back 'em off him real quick because he was blessed to be stronger than he appeared. So, a lot of white guys tried it with Dad 'cause they thought they'd win. They didn't.

At Offutt, to cool off after work, the guys would sit around and wrestle in the barracks. Now, this is the sixties, so it's exactly what you think it is. Real racist, but also, some normal people. It was all macho friendly, but one day, there was a white guy who loved to bully every minority he came in contact with. Six foot three, 240 pounds. Everyone could tell what kind of person he was, even the white people. Everyone noticed that this guy was a proud racist and no one was quite as terrible as him but no one was quite ready to tell him to eat shit. Let's call him Big Racist. Big Racist loved to pick on Dad because he's Black but mostly because Dad is half his size. So, he happened upon Dad's barracks wrestling nonsense one night. Now, this guy is humongous and sure that he could beat anyone around. He was talking trash left and right! Not the fun kind of "talking trash." The racist kind that makes everyone have a bad time. It's the one cooldown these guys have and this turd is ruining it. The white people were mad, the minorities were mad. Tension mounted and it became clear that one of these minorities would have to put him in his place. He goads Dad on. And my perfect dad, who hads been tortured by this guy for weeks at this point, realizes he is the minorities' best bet.

Aww! Dad finally has some comprehensive advertising! Dad: The minorities' best bet.

Hahahaha!! If white people have the Great White Hope, we've got Dad: The Minorities' Best Bet!

Cute!

Dad politely invites this guy to wrestle. It's Daddy versus Goliath. Word spread and people gathered to watch.

Everyone circled up because while the other matches had been for bragging rights, this one would be for equality in the barracks. Big Racist had been so terrible to all the minorities that even the white people wanted him to lose.

Same mistake Trump made.

The exact same. So, the match started and Big Racist went for an easy submission hold but Dad, who was on his high school wrestling team, slipped right out of it. This was going to be a lot harder than Big Racist thought. They went round for round but Big Racist simply could not get the best of Dad. He left, angry. And everyone had a great night. From then on, Big Racist had less respect and fewer friends. Dad received kudos from the other minorities who got to enjoy a more mellow Big Racist from then on out.

This story receives high marks for confidence. But, I like my racists to be upfront about their intentions. 5/10.

Now, this book isn't going to be a bunch of stories all willy-nilly where I just say whatever story I'm thinking of whenever I think of it no matter how little it has to do with this book, but it very is.

That Dad story kind of happened to me, too! It wasn't a racist, just a bully. The frigging biggest kid in all of high school. He looked like a grown man and was terrifying. He made fun of and bullied everyone. I had him in my study hall. Now, kids had just stopped making fun of me. It was my junior year and I had hit puberty, got braids, a new front tooth, contacts, was a cheerleader, and—this is true—teachers I had sophomore year had no clue who I was junior year.

I believe the children call it a "glow up."

So, a little parlor trick I used to have when I was young was the ability to beat anyone in arm wrestling. I guess it wasn't a trick, I was just a strong person. Gymnastics, blah, blah, blah. But one day in study hall, that bully wouldn't leave one of my little nerd buddies alone. He was gonna use the whole study hall hour to torture this kid. He was getting on the teacher's nerves and being disruptive. So, I asked the teacher if I could arm wrestle him. It was also a game day, so I was dressed in my little cheerleading outfit. I walked up to him, happy and nice. I chirped, "Betcha I can beatcha arm wrestling." He laughed so loudly the whole study hall dropped what they were doing to watch. I sat and grabbed his hand and said, "Ready?" I then made the most intense eye contact with him as I slowly pushed his hand into the table. The entire class erupted. OOOHHHHH! They all had a good laugh. I sat down. He shut up.

0/10. Off topic.

Fair.

NOSIEST NEIGHBOR

Our sister Angie was getting dropped off at our house and instead of getting out of their car right away, she and her friend sat in the driveway yapping. We don't remember how long they were in the car but, after a while Angie came in and told Dad that the police came and said they have to leave because our white lady neighbor called the cops and said— and this is real—the car looks like the car of someone she does not like. A white woman called the cops and said she didn't like the way that car looked and asked the cops to drive to our house and tell them to leave. And, and this is the crazy part, the cops said, "Okay. That's part of what we do and we are happy to oblige." They had to leave their drive-way because the neighbor didn't like that they were there. In their own driveway. A cop came to the house and made Angie leave her own driveway. Also, sidenote, Angie has had so many hilarious racist run-ins that she didn't remember this one; Dad did.

This story receives high marks for audacity but low marks for cowardice. Bring your raggedy behind over here and tell Angie to leave to her face! 5/10.

Mommy is a little smarty-pants. If you read the last book, you're all like, "Quit referencing it!" But also, if you read the last book, you may remember Mommy skipped second and seventh grade. Anyhoo, this isn't a story about how smart my mom is. Wait, actually I do have one:

When I was in school, I sucked a butt at math. Like, I was failing remedial math. Technically, I should not have graduated from high school, but I was really nice and tried hard so, for once, I got preferential treatment. I guess I get it all the time now, but back then? Never. Anyway, I would ask Mom for help with my homework, and she would just know the answer. Like, she would just know when John Quincy Adams was president or she'd take one look at a math problem and blurt out the answer. It was very cool. But that's not the story.

WORST LETTER

The story is when Mom worked at the downtown bank, Omaha National, the only other employee of color was another Black woman named Barb. Their white supervisor hated their guts. Dirty looks, ignoring them completely, giving them extra work, the whole nine. If they were all in a room, he would make sure to speak to everyone but Barb and Mom. Okay fine. Mom's had worse. She can make this work. Now, one of the things they had to do in this job was find errors in totals. You had to balance checks. It's not the easiest job for most people, but it just so happens that my math-y mom is excelling at it. Mom was doing better than everyone else there. So much so that she spent time helping people. At two different bank locations she was doing the work of her supervisor. And at the same time, they wanted her to maintain her own quota. So, she had to do not only her job, but also her supervisor's work, too. Long after it should have, the workload becomes more than she can handle. Also, the very same people whose work she is doing are filing complaints about her.

Mom had no choice. She went to the president of the bank and told on her supervisor. This bold little mommy went to the president of the whole dang bank and he was like, "We will take care of that." He took care of that by telling the supervisor, who immediately called her into his office to say, "Don't ever do that again." So, the supervisors got together and typed up a letter for her and told her "Sign this letter or leave."

Here is Lacey's best recollection of the letter:

Dear White Leaders,

My apologies. I am but a Negress, a whiz with a calculator, but too smart for my own good. How dare I be so smart and so dang cute? Who the butt do I think I am? How dare I call you out for being bad at your jobs while doing your jobs for you?! This is poop and I'm one bad little lady.

Okay, I just found out Lacey has never seen the letter.

But the letter was racist and inflammatory and basically said, "Know your place." Mom, having no clue what the fuck place that was, immediately walked out but she made sure to take the letter. She went home and found out she was pregnant with her first baby, Chrystal! It would only take four babies for Mom and Dad to finally get it right. So, Mom applied for unemployment. The person in the unemployment office didn't want to give her unemployment because "It's okay for people to talk to you like that." Can you believe that? What's that? You can? I know. But she kept that letter and made copies of it and sent it to the state Equal Employment Opportunity Commission. And you'll never believe this part. The EEOC sent someone out to Omaha! They sent a Black lawyer to represent Mom. He was perfect and attentive and won the case! Mom got a year's pay! Hahahahaha. Please let that victory sink in before this, the end of the story: The Black guy who represented Mom saw her again years later. When Mom thanked him for all his help, he told her it was his honor. He also let her know that pushing for Mom's investigation and winning her case cost him his job! Fighting for justice cost him his job at the EEO motherfucking C. Unbelievable.

10/10. This competition is over. There are more stories to come. In fact, the majority of our stories are to come. But I'm gonna stop this competition here because this story really hurt my little feelings.

This man lost his job helping Mom.

Can you stand it?

I cannot.

10/10.

For sure 10/10.

WORST DONATIONS

It should not surprise you to find out that Mom was the first Black president of the PTA at our elementary school. One of her duties in that position was fundraising. There was a list of donors, usually businesses that would donate a hefty sum to the school each year. So, Mom is working her way down this list. On it was one of the banks whose name is on all the banners at school, so she knows they're gonna give her a lot. Mom gets to the bank president's office and told them she was the PTA president. They laughed in her face. They didn't believe her.

Faking being the president of the PTA is the most boring grift I could ever think of. Wanna seduce an old widow? Nope. Wanna rob a store? Nope. I wanna pretend to be a PTA president.

And when she insisted it was true, these people offered the wildest donation of all time. They reached up onto the shelf into a box of pencils that was among many other boxes of pencils and scooped up twelve pencils and handed them to Mom. Not money. Not boxes of pencils, not one box of pencils but twelve pencils OUT OF A BOX OF PENCILS.

MOST RACIST DOG

Directly behind the backyard of the house we all grew up in is a big field with a church on the other side. One time when Jimmy was four or so, Dad and he cut across the field behind our house to get gas for the lawn mower. But, the church behind our house had construction workers there, rebuilding a part of the building. With them was a giant dog. As they were walking across the field, the dog attacked. Dad had Jimmy and the gas can, so he was swinging Jimmy in one hand and swinging the gas can in the other. He was trying to keep Jimmy safe and fight the dog off with the gas can. He finally fought the dog off and he looks up and the construction workers were just standing there watching. They just watched as their dog attacked a dad and his little boy. Jimmy asked what was wrong with that dog. Isn't that story just the worst? To watch a guy and his little baby fight off your dog. Motherfuckers are so lucky Dad is so chill.

> **Dad:** So anyway, for whatever that story
> is worth.

He's so cute.

MOST IMPROVED RACIST

Chrystal, my oldest sister, and I had the same kindergarten teacher. When Chrystal had her, she was terrible. But by the time I had her, she was so super nice. I could read in kindergarten, and she would show me off constantly. This woman loved me so bad. She was thrilled with every last bit of work I did. She would slip me harder work on the sly. She would ask me challenging questions while asking the other kids regular ones. Just to see what my limits were. It was the most preferential treatment I have ever had. She loved me so bad that she never put up any of my drawings. She did this because she praised me constantly and tried to make up for it by praising the other kids for their artwork. Even I could see that at five.

Now, I don't know what happened in those eight or so

years but when Chrystal had her, the teacher was acting wild. When it was time for recess, she claimed she couldn't button Chrystal's jacket 'cause it was "too complicated." Bitch! It's BUTTONS! So, during winter recess, she would have someone come in and do it for her so she wouldn't have to touch Chrystal. Chrystal was just five and couldn't quite tie her shoes and whenever she needed help, the teacher would ask someone else to do it. But, and you already know this, if a white kid needed help with their shoes, she would do it. But the real story is this: Okay, so do you know square dancing? Like when people put on cowboy boots and frilly skirts and whip each other around to fiddle music? Well, you know that part of it where everyone trades partners and moves around in a circle? You know, you separate for a second and come back to your partner and it's someone else. Okay, you get it. So, Chrystal's class square-danced for the school show. It was adorable and as my parents watched, they realized something. Chrystal had one other Black kid in her class. A boy. And when their class did the square dance for their parents, somehow, in the middle of a sea of white children constantly changing partners, Chrystal and the other Black kid only ever touched each other.

Oh my god. I never realized this. You know what must've happened? Mom! I would bet a million dollars Mom said something to her that really hurt her feelings or scared her into gradually treating each Ruffin child better than the last.

I cannot believe I lived all these years thinking it was some sort of grand mystery when Mom is literally RIGHT THERE.

Mom is the reason Black children are being treated right. OOH! That's two!

Dad: The minorities' best bet!

And Mom: The reason Black children are being treated right.

MOST RACIST APARTMENT BUILDING

In 1966 my parents moved from Offutt Air Force Base into the city of Omaha. At this time there weren't many nice places where Black people could live. So, Mom and Dad got a real estate broker. They promptly showed Mom and Dad all the worst places in town because they're Black. They would have to do their own searching. As Mom and Dad are looking for a place, they wander to the edge of what a lot of people would call the Black neighborhood back then. It was a neighborhood that wasn't all the way Black yet but was starting to turn Black. They found a For Rent sign on a nice building at Sixteenth and Lake. Bretnor Terrace Apartments. They knock on the door and see that it is owned by two white people. They hesitantly showed them the apartment. It was, to not quote my parents, the shit. Mom and Dad told the owners they were interested. The owners exchanged a glance, heaved a heavy sigh, and took them to their home and sat them down. They said, "If we let you move into this area, the white people will move out. We need you to give us a commitment to tell people at Offutt that your landlords are good to colored people." It was a fully furnished nice apartment. Satin drapes and sheets. Nicer than anything they'd ever seen. Now, here in this book, I've edited it down quite a bit but, rest assured, this woman cooked and fed us a whole dinner before she was done telling us about how nice this place was. Mom and Dad said they would be happy to spread the word for them. They got the apartment. The price of rent they saw on the sign was of course less than they paid (we will be getting into Black Tax later when Lacey goes to a car dealership) but they didn't mind because they've been Black since time began so they knew they were going to get overcharged. Mom was fine with paying the Black Tax. She accepted it because, and she'll tell you as much, THE PLACE WAS SO NICE.

The Black Tax turned out to be more than money. Anytime Mom and Dad saw one of the other tenants, the tenants would turn their back on them. As if to dare them to knife them in the kidney. Just kidding. They did knife a few, though. Just kidding.

But it was a long time before all the white people moved out. So, things got worse for a while. Mom and Dad parked in the lot behind the building. It was their normal parking spot. Their new neighbors threw dirt and rocks on the hood and caused $300 worth of damage to their car. That was their way of letting them know they did not want Mom and Dad in their neighborhood. It did not work.

As we are talking to Mom and Dad, it's becoming clear that they remember different things because of how it hit them at the time. You know? Like, there may be some incidents nowhere near as bad as Lacey's but because of what the fucking world was back then, it hit them differently. And there's always a variable of like, what the rest of your frigging day was. So, Lacey decided to ask them a more specific question:

EARLIEST RACIST MEMORY—THE DAD CATEGORY

Just for the opposite of fun, we asked Mom and Dad what their first memory of racism is. Dad grew up in Portsmouth, Virginia. When he was four, his mom worked for some white people. Dad and his family lived in a house in low-income housing and these people she worked for were less than a block away in the white neighborhood. "The white family's kid would come over and play and one day her mom caught her and told my mom that she couldn't play with us anymore. That's the first time I remember there being a difference between people."

EARLIEST RACIST MEMORY—THE MOM CATEGORY

Mom's first racist memory is downtown Savannah, Georgia, on Broughton Street. Downtown in general. "If you went downtown to go to the store and buy stuff, you weren't allowed to eat at the counter in a store. You couldn't get food anywhere downtown and if you had it, you couldn't eat it. Not only would they not serve you food, you couldn't ask for food. You could use the bathroom, but only the ones for Black people. It was extremely unfair because you could shop and they'd take your money, but when it came time to check out, you had to wait and let any white people, whether they were behind you or not go first. So, on a busy day, you just had to stand in line and anytime a white person felt like it, they could hop in line in front of you." This is a detail that dropped my jaw. I had just never thought about this, but of course white people would just cut you in line. Some motherfuckers do that shit now! Can you imagine what that would do to the Black people who had to endure that unfairness daily? Can you imagine what that would do to the white people? Maaaan. Getting cut in line is maddening to me. And now I know my hate for this was passed down from my ancestors. If you have ever seen someone who looked like me at a FedEx cussing out an old white lady who cut her, IT WAS AND FOREVER WILL BE ME. And I say "just kidding" way too many times in this book but I need you to note how I did not put that phrase here 'cause I'm dead serious 'cause it has happened two full times at the FedEx by the park in Midtown Manhattan. Full volume cussing a bitch the fuck out.

You use too much foul language. I'd like Mom and Dad to note how few cuss words I've used and how many Amber has used. It is because she is bad and I am good.

Parents, my very old sister is right. I vow right here, right now, not to use any more curse words in this book.

MOST RACIST BUS RIDE

In college, Mom had to catch the bus to university to take classes during the summer. But Mom graduated from high school when she was sixteen, and is a small person, so people thought she was just a little girl. Because she was Black and alone, they would say, "So, you're going to summer school, huh? Flunking out?" Mom explained you couldn't take summer school classes to catch up, you could only take them as extra credit. No one believed her. Every day she'd get on the bus and every day she'd explain herself. And every day they'd say, "That's a lie." And she finally started just agreeing with everyone who said she was on her way to summer school. She realized it would be easier to let them think a lie than to convince them of the truth.

This reminds me of this one Lacey story. Please keep in mind that this is our mom so we are allowed to make hard left turns like this:

A million years ago, when our niece Jazmyn was a little kid we were all at our parents' house and Lacey asked Jazmyn how old she was. Jazmyn replied, "four." And that simply was not true. So, Lacey explained to Jazmyn she was mistaken about her age. She was three. But Jazmyn was having none of it. We don't like lying little children in our family so Lacey tried again to tell her that she was three. Jazmyn got angry. Lacey let her know that her attitude would not be tolerated and gave her a long lecture that ended with Lacey saying, "Now, how old are you, Jazmyn?" and Jazmyn finally admitting, "I'm three." Chrystal, Jazmyn's mom, came home and confirmed Jazmyn was indeed four.

And now, in our family, anytime someone gives up you say, "I'm three."

EARLIEST RACE WAR

When Dad was like twelve, he lived right on the border between a Black and a white neighborhood. And what bordered the both of them was a Navy shipyard. The shipyard workers would park their cars in a lot that was several blocks long and wide. The whole thing was gravel and therefore an endless supply of rocks. Because Dad's area bordered the white area, there was always a confrontation. And, and this blew my mind, they used to have rock fights there! The white kids and the Black kids would have rock fights. Someone would call someone a name and the rock fight would begin! Just twelve-year-old white and Black kids fucking hurling rocks at each other! Can you stand it? If any one of those white kids had lost an eye, who knows what would have happened! Bad dad. My dad was bad.

While talking to Mom and Dad about all this, Dad said something I had never thought about. He told me about how, in school, they were segregated. His whole life, he never went to school with white kids. He talked about how well-behaved and whip smart the Black kids he went to school with were. When he got to Omaha, he noticed the Black kids weren't excelling like they did back home. They were getting in trouble for misbehaving a lot. He said that this was happening because they go to classes taught by white people with white students and the white students get preferential treatment.

The Black children are also probably explicitly told they are not as smart. (I know I was told as much!) Meanwhile, to become a teacher when you're Black, even if you taught at an all-Black school (which was your only option) Black teachers had to be overqualified. They also saw the true potential of Black children and treated Black kids as if they were smart, so they got a better education. This is the closest my dad will ever come to shit talking.

Then, Dad said something else I'd never thought of before.

Dad says, "It was understood that when we got on the bus, Black people just moved to the back. I went into the military after high school and can't pinpoint the transition but things changed. For me, I always felt like if whites didn't want me around them, my attitude was I didn't want to be around them. I certainly wasn't gonna try to make it happen. But a lot of Black people felt differently. They wanted to force the white people into integration. I was content to leave it the way it was as long as I had equal opportunities. But I came to realize, you can't have segregation and equality. This is easier to see once you have kids. 'Resa* and I realized that once you have kids, you get mad for them. You realize there isn't anything in this world they don't have a right to. You get to be more defensive, and you stand up for your rights."

I do like yelling out "'Resa!" in the store when we get separated even though I always get in trouble.

---

* Dad sometimes calls Mom, Theresa, by his nickname for her, 'Resa. When we feel like getting in trouble, we will also call Mom 'Resa. It's hilarious when you're doing it but never worth the consequences. That's why I'm shocked that Lacey typed this. How could she? Little troublemaker.

Another way we like to earn a whoopin' is me and Lacey's favorite game:

So, whenever we are at Mom and Dad's, we go into the kitchen while Mom is cleaning. She instantly does not want you there, but as her child, it's your job to make things worse. When Mom is in the kitchen cleaning and you pour yourself and Lacey tea in a wineglass—it's on. When this happens, Lacey and I start talking like we are superrich white people. We will put on silly voices and it'll be like:

"Oh, I just love this yacht. Is it new?"

"Of course. I wouldn't be caught dead in an old yacht!"

"Caviar?"

"Thank you. Put it on my diamond-studded plate."

Now, Mom knows what's about to happen, but technically, she can't get mad until we've done it. We will talk for a while, jockeying for first position to leave the kitchen and be the farthest from Mom's reach. And then, when you think you're safe, you point at Mom and try to be the first to blurt out:

"Ewww. Your help is making eye contact with me."

Then, you bolt like your life depends on it 'cause Mom is gonna getcha.

GREAT-GRANDMA'S WORST STORY

Mom's grandmother. The police came into her neighborhood for some bogus reason or another, when in reality, they were just looking for someone to harass. This was (and in many places still is) a regular thing. They found Mom's grandma. They twisted her wrist and broke her watch and put her in jail. Her family bailed her out. When she went to court, it was understood she had to say nothing and be remorseful. And she was and they let her go. And when they did, she said, "God ain't dead," and they put her back in jail for saying it. Isn't that a crazy, shitty thing to have to live with?

Amber said she wouldn't cuss and she lied.

They knew it was a lie the second I said it.

Another fun fact that came up while talking to Mom and Dad is something I'd never thought of—Black police were not allowed to arrest white people. Like, they had gone through the same classes but couldn't arrest the same people. Again, it makes sense once you take a look at this country but dang! I never knew this! You just know those Black cops heard all kinds of crap.

MOST OVERZEALOUS COP

When Dad was a freshman in high school, he was walking home from school. He was a block and a half from his house.

Clear across town the cops were looking for a Black teen-ager who had allegedly snatched a purse. And you already know. Somehow, two white cops end up looking in Dad's neighborhood and see Dad walking down the street. They grab him and put him in the car. They take Dad clear across town not to arrest him but to bring him directly to the house of the woman with the stolen purse. They get Dad out of the car and walk him up to the door. The door opens and the family comes out. Luckily there was a girl in there who knew Dad from school and she said, "That's not him. How did you even get him? That's James, he lives all the way across town!"

At this point, Dad reveals he's never been fired from a job and receives quite a razzing included but not limited to:

"Do I have to tell people my dad is white?"

"How are we even related?!"

"Are you sure you ever **had** a job?"

"If you've never been fired, how did you know when it was time to change jobs?"

"Sad to have a Dad who tells lies."
And so on.

WORST SERVICE STORIES—THE MOM CATEGORY

Traveler's Checks

Okay so, a million years ago there were these things called traveler's checks. They were like money you could travel with that, if stolen, could be replaced. Mom always got her traveler's checks from the same place, from the same woman who would, while giving her a dirty look, just throw five twenties on the counter and walk away.

Gas

Mom and Dad move into a new house and need to have the gas turned on. So, Mom calls Acme, and they send someone out. This guy is unhappy to be there. There's this thing where when you need work done on your house or car, sometimes the person they send you is sad that they, even for this little bit of time, have to "work for" a Black person. You can watch them angrily search for a way to get their dignity back. It's gross and sad and still happening. OH MY GOD IT'S HAPPENING RIGHT NOW.

Okay so, as we are writing this story down, it's me and Lacey at Mom and Dad's. We are sitting in the living room writing down our parents' stories. Last night, they had a blockage in the drain and the basement flooded with sewage. So today, we called a plumber to fix it. When he gets here, he has the look. He's mad, y'all. So, we bring him downstairs and ask him all the questions we think he can bear before it's clear he needs to be left alone.

At one point, I go back down the stairs, walk up to him to ask another question, and he tells me to get out of his way because he is holding something heavy. "Get out of my way" in **my** house. Yes, he did.

He keeps complaining about how terrible the blockage is and how hard it is to find and get to. So, in order to get to the problem, he has to, in his waterproof plumber boots, step on the wet floor. He does this and also needs to go back and forth to his truck a lot. He tracks sewage up and down the carpeted steps. We think, *Oh well, we will just have to replace that along with all the damaged carpet in the basement. Too bad there's nothing we could put down.*

I ask him how long until I can tell the cleanup guys to come. He says, "I can't call the cleanup people for you. It doesn't work like that, I just get rid of the blockage and—" I interrupt him and say, "I don't need help finding a person. I'm on the phone with them now. If you tell me when you'll be done, I can let them know when to come over, you griping ass bitch." Okay, I don't say that last part but he says, "Oh, I'm almost done now!" Little idiot.

Then, Will from 1-800-WATER DAMAGE comes over, kind as hell, and puts down plastic wrap on the steps while he works, so as not to track the sewage everywhere. I just so happen to get a look in the back of the plumber's giant truck, and there isn't a doubt in my mind that he has that plastic in there but simply chose not to use it. This is happening as we are writing this story down! That guy is so lucky we aren't allowed to talk shit about specific people or businesses. It's a shame 'cause I want to warn Black people not to have that company in your house. Guess you'll just have to privately ask me. But you know who you should call? Will from 1-800-WATER-DAMAGE. What a little angel. Anyways, let me get back to the story!

So, Mom's pregnant and in the new house. Acme sends a guy to turn on the gas. This man arrived mad and stayed mad. He's a giant white guy. As he's checking the pilot light, he's using matches, trying to see if it'll take. The match goes out, and he throws it on the floor and lights a new match. Mom was home alone and is watching him throw matches on the floor. He's watching her watching him. They share a look where he knows what he's doing and she knows he knows. Gross. I bet a million dollars that that man went on to have a son who was a plumber 'cause dang.

MOST RACIST BOUTIQUE

Once, when Chrystal was a toddler, Mom saw a tiny cute baby boutique was having a sale. On their door they have the list of credit cards they accept. It's every credit card. Mom checks the list and notices they accept hers. She walked in, did some shopping, walked up to the register with some clothes, and the man behind the counter said, "We do not accept credit cards." Now, at a major chain, it's worth it to make a stink. They certainly have policies in place, and they want that money. So, anyone acting crazy can be fired. But at a small boutique like this, the person you're talking to is likely the owner and putting money into that business is likely going to a true piece of shit. She leaves.

Not a full new chapter but definitely a page break, mutha-fuckas! 'Cause it's time for some shit that blew my mind:

THE

JCPENNEY

ORIGINAL

STORY!!

In the last book we had a whole chapter about how Lacey was forever followed around at JCPenney.

Well, like mother like daughter because Mom was followed around JCPenney, too!

Mom used to wear this really cute leather cape. It was a hard-to-explain cape-y shawl thing. Like a short poncho. It was so cute, and I have no clue where that ended up. If I found it, I would wear it tomorrow, and you would be gagging.

Sidenote: Mom will dress OUT. She used to make her own clothes and, in the seventies, was quite the fashion plate.

So, every time Mom would come to JCPenney in this cape, they'd follow her. She'd buy whatever merchandise she came to buy and walk out to the van and every time, there was a guy watching her who had followed her out to the parking lot waiting to see if she took out anything from her shirt. I asked her if she ever took out two middle fingers and showed him those. I got in trouble.

So, years before I was followed around that store for years, Mom was followed around that store for years. She woulda told us sooner but, and this is important, SHE FORGOT. That's the number of stories we are dealing with.

While sitting around with Mom and Dad, it occurred to us that they have a lot of experience dealing with racist incidents at stores and stuff, so we thought we'd share some of their expertise with you!

I asked Mom and Dad how to properly file a complaint and Amber ruined it. Here you go:

How to Properly File a Complaint—by Mom and Dad

> *Mom:* When people are disrespectful—
> *Amber:* Like Lacey.
> *Mom:* —you can try to resolve it with
> them, but you may not be able to.
> *Amber:* 'Cause some people are un-
> reasonable, like Lacey.

Mom: So, you're going to go to customer service. And tell them what happened.
Amber: So, it'll be something like, "Your worker is not only gross to look at but rude and smelly. I think her name is Lacey."
Dad: Customer service will tell you who is responsible for the person. And, if they don't, you gotta start asking for supervisors. You have to make sure to let them know exactly what happened and exactly why it's inappropriate.
Amber: So, that would be like, "I need to talk to you about your smelliest employee." And they would reply, "Lacey? She's just a weirdo who wandered in here."

I can't stand my baby sister sometimes.

CHAPTER FOUR

WHY DON'T YOU BELIEVE ME?

T his is not the time for this, but I just remembered another
song we used to sing. This is from when I was very, very
little and I thought I had written a hit.

You mean WE had written a hit, stop trying to steal my
thunder.

♪♪I saw the pony climb up the tree
I saw the pony and the pony saw me
But when the pony said stop, I didn't stop
So he hit me on the head with his clippity clop♪♪

MOST UNBELIEVABLE STORY

Okay, so you know how white people will try to strike up a
conversation with Black people by bringing up anything they
think of as a "Black" subject? Sometimes people even tell you

71

whole stories about their Black friend. Well, there's also this phenomenon of making up stories for their own clout. Like, it makes them seem cool to you or your friends. Or—and this is so hyper-specific to being the only Black person at work—they tell a made-up story to a big bunch of your coworkers while you're standing right there. The story is essentially about how bad or dangerous Black people are. I assume their goal in this is to get all your coworkers to say, "Yeah, Black people are bad." Or something along those lines. It has for sure happened to me before, but my memory is not as good as Lacey's nor was I keeping a handy-dandy journal!

Wait! Let's play a game! Okay, do you remember a show called *Beyond Belief: Fact or Fiction*? It was my favorite! It was hosted by Jonathan Frakes from *Star Trek* and the premise was this: Every show they'd reenact five or so stories. All of them were impossible to believe! Then, at the end of the show, they'd tell you which ones were true and which ones were false. It would blow your mind! Let's do that with these stories! Okay? Okay!

In my Best Jonathan Frakes voice

You are about to hear three stories; some are true and some are false. It will be up to you to use logic and deductive reasoning, but I don't know if that will help you because these stories are truly . . . BEYOND BELIEF.

Story one: At work one day, at none other than the worst place on earth—the morning meeting—my least favorite coworker is trying to strike up a conversation with me. She's a "your hair is gross" type of racist. Which is an entire genre of racism. Her exact quote is: "Did you know that a lot of times Black people have spiders in their braids?" I'll give you a million dollars if you can guess how my hair was when she said that! Anyhoo, this lady asks me about my book during the meeting, and I let her know it's about the racism I have encountered here in Omaha. She then says, "Well, I have a story for you, then." *Wow, you have a story? You have a story about racism in Omaha? Bitch, is it about you and your mouth?!* But I don't say that out loud. Out loud I say, "Great, let's hear it." She begins to tell me how she went on vacation with her Black boyfriend to visit his family. Okay, so this has nothing to do with Omaha but oh well, let's hear about the racism. Again, I'm the only Black person in the meeting; there is no one I can turn to that will understand my pain. She tells me she was the only white person in this town she visited, and it was terrifying. She says her boyfriend introduced her to a lot of interesting and dangerous characters. They're all hanging outside on the front porch of this house when a van pulls up to a young man who is walking down the sidewalk. The van door slides open. It's full of gang members! They shout at the young man. "Aye! You got our stuff, youngblood?" The boy says "Naw, man. I ain't got it." The van of gang members say, "We will give you till the count of five to try to run. Then, we're gonna kill you." She has the wide eyes and frantic pace of a liar. And the more I look at her with a face that says, *We all know this is a lie*, the more she amps up the story. Everyone, "Run, boy, run!" The boy takes off down the street, and they chase him. She says she hears gunshots and then silence. Everyone just goes back to normal talking and socializing as if nothing happened. "That's how normal it is for them!" I ask her, So you saw his body in the street? Did anyone call the police, did anyone help? She says no. Okay, there are so many ways that this story has nothing to do with racism in Omaha. I tell you what my book is about, and this is the story you tell me?! Let's say every single thing you have told me is true, and, just so we are all on the same page here, there is no way it could possibly be, how is this related to my book, and why did you choose this time and place to share it? Were you trying to give me another story for this book? 'Cause you did, you ignorant fool.

Story two: When we were young and fun, my friend was friends with a guy who was a country music DJ, and he was a million different kinds of bad. Once he came to pick up my friend at my house. This neighborhood is not bad. Especially back then. But it was technically on "the bad side of town," so white people who were never over there really lost their minds about it because of assumptions they'd come to. So, this guy gets to our house and, in an effort to prove god knows what to me, launches into a story about how he actually *liked* this neighborhood. I mean, you lost me before you started but do continue. He says, "I'm blasting my country music at the stoplight down the street, I pull up next to these two Black guys. They're blasting music, too. It's rap. Now these are some pretty tough-looking guys. They give me a dirty look and turn their music up. So, I turn my music up. This goes back and forth until they finally give up and the two Black guys go 'You know what, man, you're all right.'" Now, aside from being the dumbest thing I've ever heard, it's also impossible. How could he have heard them with the music all the way up? Also who in their right mind would do any of this? The answer is no one because it never happened. Fucking idiot.

Story three: I once had a boss who fully supported me and was zero percent problematic.

Are you ready for the answers? What's that? True, true, false? You got it right! Your prize is whatever's in your pocket! Yay!

And now a story about our lovable brother Jimmy!

JIMMY IN COUNCIL BLUFFS

Jimmy and I had a song we used to sing that I've only heard stories about. It was when we were very, very small.

I had nothing to do with this one.

It went like this:

♪♪Video lady. Video man. Video lady. Video lady. Video man.♪♪

Not a top-ten hit but it definitely would be played on house music night.

Okay, so our brother Jimmy is not a huge fan of ours because we always bother him and talk over him and tell him he's a little baby. Well, we stayed quiet for about twenty minutes after asking, "Hey, Jimmy. You got any racist stories?" and he told us this:

MOST RACIST PARKING LOT

When he was young and just out of high school, our brother Jimmy had a friend who lived in Council Bluffs for a small tortured amount of time. It did not last long. Once they went to the grocery store and Jimmy noticed people hanging out in the parking lot.

Sidenote: That's how you know you're in a small town. When people are just hanging in the local grocery store parking lot.

So, on their way out, they stopped to talk to the parking lot crowd and a cop car drove up to Jimmy and told only him to "go back where you came from." In Council Bluffs, them cops ain't subtle.

MOST RACIST GAS STATION

Once, while in Council Bluffs, Jimmy walked to the gas station. On his way home, the cops were called on him. Six cop cars pull up to him and flash their lights. The cops tell him to "stop moving." They get out of their cars and all but one of the cops unholsters their weapons. Someone had called the cops because they "saw a suspicious person in the neighborhood." Guys. Someone called the cops on Jimmy for being Black outside. Just being around. Good god. Jimmy explained how he was just walking back to his friend's place after making a trip to the gas station. One of the cops said, "If I was you, I'd hurry home before it gets worse."

RUNNERS-UP

At a different gas station in Council Bluffs, he was told, "Your kind is not welcome here."

At his friend's friend's house in Council Bluffs, the dad came home and said, "What is this n-word doing in my house? They steal. You can't be here."

Now, here's the thing. All these things happened to him in Council Bluffs. I was pulled over by a man I thought was gonna kill me in Council Bluffs (it's in the first book), and Lacey almost froze to death in a car while an insane person watched her from his van in Council Bluffs (also in the first book). BUT Council Bluffs has quite the brunch scene. There's a place on Broadway that has really fun drag brunch and it seems safe enough and the menu looks fucking legit but I don't want to go. Everyone, pick a side and tell Lacey why it's mine.

I apologize for her rude behavior, it's one of my favorite places now and she's definitely going.

Edit: Oh no. I went and had fun. If we get killed by cops in Council Bluffs, know that it was for brunch!

CHAPTER FIVE

DON'T GO IN THAT STORE

I t's always nice paying actual money to be someone's racist experiment. You walk into a store and you walk out with a new understanding of how terrible the world is. Here are the winners for:

WORST CAR SERVICE

I was on my way to the airport so I decided to take an Uber there. I use Uber all the time in New York, but it is nothing like Omaha, I mean not even close. More times than not, I get the most interesting driver you can imagine. This time my driver was an older white woman. As I get into her car she immediately changes the station from easy rock to the rap station. This also happens all the time. It's sad I'm so used to it. As the music is playing she raises her voice so I can hear her. (Hey, how about just turning the music down?) Anyway this woman says, "You know, my boyfriend says that you guys are all on CP time but not you! You came out right away! So I guess not all colored people are late. Oh my boyfriend is Black by the way." Really? Why didn't he teach you not to repeat that phrase? You were dumb enough to actually say "CP time" and then made it worse by saying "colored people"? Did you know that there is a way you can complain about your driver? Did you know that it's next to impossible to get a response? Now, having taken these cars everywhere, I can tell you they should already have a canned response they send to everyone who complains.

Here! I'll even write it for you:

Dear [customer name],

We are sorry about the racism you experienced while being trapped in the car with a stranger. It is unacceptable behavior for the driver to have [touched your hair/called you colored/gone on and on about how poor people are just lazy]. Although it makes for a good story, we feel bad about it. The driver will receive a sternly worded email.

Have fun deleting our app in anger and then re-downloading it!

Love,
UBER

MOST RACIST CAR DEALERSHIP

Welcome to my least favorite story of the book. You know how in the first book there were a few stories that bothered you after you read them? Well this one bothers theeeee literal fuck outta me. I swear to God. Okay so, Lacey was looking for a new car recently, and she knew it was going to be a bad experience. It always is. As she was talking to her friend about this, she says, "My son just got a job at a really nice dealership! He'll give you a good deal!" Lacey is thrilled to be able to buy a car from someone she knows. And, it'll be the first time she gets to buy a car from a Black person! Sweet.

So, she gets to the dealership, looks around for like forty-five minutes and sees a car she likes! She and her friend's son go over the price, and Lacey asks if they can do better if she pays in cash. Her friend's son says, "Absolutely! Let me talk to my manager." Now, we've all been here before. Lacey's sitting in the waiting area, but she can hear them talking. She heard the manager say, "Do you know her?" and her friend says, "Yes!" Then the manager replies, "Oh. Okay." The friend's son calls Lacey over. She walks up to the manager who says to her, "Why do you want to pay cash? Why don't you just get a loan?" Uh-oh. He's rude. Lacey replies, "'Cause I'm not." The man asks, "What do you even do?" Lacey says, "I write." That's vague as hell but that's all he's getting. He then tells her that cash won't make the price any better but if she were to get a loan, they could take off $1,800. They were not willing to budge a penny. Not a penny! Now, we know too many people with cars to not be aware of what is happening here.

And I will say that I had the same experience buying my car in upstate New York. The dealership had a gigantic "Blue Lives Matter" flag, and I shoulda left right then. We offered cash, they offered us money off to take a loan, and would not come down one dollar on the cash price. I said, "Under no circumstances will I ever be getting a loan I don't need. That's not how money works." And yes, I was rude. I was so mad that I would have happily driven a shittier car forever just to spite them. But my husband really wanted it. So, we got it. I'm ashamed. Comfortable and ashamed.

So, once they say they can't come down on the price, Lacey's like, "Okay. Thanks." And turns around to leave. As she's walking out she thanks the young man, and he seems a bit embarrassed but it's not his fault. As soon as Lacey gets into her car, she calls our white male family friend Jim. She tells him everything that's happened. She asks if he would be able to come to the dealership and look at the same car, offer cash, and tell her what they say. He says, "I'm on my way."

He lives for this stuff!

Now, if you've read the first book, you already know this is something Lacey does a lot. She sends Jim into a place she suspects is being racist and all of a sudden, they DO have apartments available or room for appointments or doughnuts.

By the time Lacey gets back home, Jim calls. He had showed up at the exact same dealership, looked at the exact same car, but with a different white salesman. He is given the same price. But when this white man says to them, "I'm paying in cash, can you do better?" Reader? Guess how much they take off. $500? $2,000? No, they take off $4,000. Hahahahaha! Four fucking thousand dollars. And I tell you the fresh rage I feel when I type this. One, because who knows how much I coulda got off my car. And two, you just KNOW these are the same motherfuckers who are like, "Black people need to pull themselves up by the bootstraps," while at the same time, locking them into debt and charging them up the ass.

Lacey finds out all of this. So, her friend's son at the dealership calls her and he tells her, "You gotta hurry back in here. There's someone looking at the car." Lacey tells him that is her friend, and they gave him a very big discount. "Whoa. Let me talk to my bosses about it." Lacey says, "Look, man. Do not get in trouble about this. It is not worth it. I do not know your position at work. Don't mess around and get in trouble." But being the complete perfect angel he is, he insists on talking to them. They end up saying, "Okay fine. We can take $1,800 off. The same price you would have gotten if you had done a loan." THEEEEESE BITCHES!! Not even the full four thousand! And if this is confusing you, you are right. Lacey knows about the $4,000 discount and they know she knows and yet they refused to give it to her. Isn't that amazing? That's how comfortable they were overcharging her. Now, Lacey did not end up buying this car. And it's at this point I want to put these motherfuckers on BLAST. But legally, we cannot do that. But if you know us and want to buy a car in Omaha, or upstate New York, please call us first.

WORST CAR REPAIR SHOP

I had taken my car in to get new tires. I dropped my car off and they were gonna call me when it was done. I get a phone call that my car is ready and I go to pick it up. As I enter the lobby there is a white woman in front of me. She walks up to the cashier and says, "My car is ready; it's right out front," and gives her name. The man gives her the keys, hands her the receipt, and she leaves. Okay, that seems easy enough. I walk up, give my name, and say, "That's my Mini Cooper right out front." The man looks bewildered, and I can tell this is going to be a shit show. "What more do you need? My name should be in the computer alongside the description of my car." How many people steal cars this way, by knowing the driver's name, but, oh well here we go. He says, "Yeah, are you at the right place? I don't think your car is here." Let me repeat that, he said, "I don't think your car is here." How many times has this happened since you worked here? How many people are dropping their cars off and then going to the wrong location to pick it up? Now there are people waiting in the lobby and they are watching, I turned to them and ask, "Did you see how easy the lady before me got her car? Why is this so hard?" I turn back to him and say, "Do you need my ID? I see my keys right behind you. What's the problem?" He is now in the computer clickety-clackin' away, and I just say I need to see a supervisor. He actually calls for one and this guy comes out and backs up his employee. "My name is Lacey Lamar. My car is right there. My keys are right there. Give me my car." "Ma'am, when did you bring this car in? You brought it here?" Now if you are in the lobby watching this unfold, I might seem like the weird lady who is trying to steal a car. I have no idea what these people are thinking, and I can't believe the amount of time it's taking for them to figure it out. I see the guy's name tag. "Randy? Randy, I talked to you this morning, you tried to upsell me on my tires for my Mini Cooper, do you remember that?" I know he has to but he is not backing down. He is not budging and had made the decision to go down with the ship. "Why don't you just use my keys, open the car door, and look at the registration?" I don't have time for this. And just like that they figure it out. Instead of asking me over and over if I was in the right place, why not assume the customer is right? I truly think they thought I just walked in off the street and tried to claim a car I saw in their parking lot. As Laurel and Hardy hand me my keys MY NAME is written on a tag attached to them. The name that I gave them, the name that would have matched the driver's license I offered to show them. But they were so panicked that they might have a Mini Cooper thief on their hands all logic went out the window. I drove my car into the building, and it burned down. JKJKJKJK.

MOST RACIST DRESS STORE

So Amber is visiting me in Omaha, and we decided to go wedding-dress shopping. Her wedding is in a few months. She's not looking for anything too over the top and really just wants an elegant, classy evening dress. I tell her I knew the perfect place. At the time I'm working at a high-end boutique at Regency Mall on the weekends, but there is an amazing dress shop right down the hall that has the perfect dress. Now, the store owner sees me almost every time I work. She walks past the store to get to her boutique and always stops by to talk. I need to make this clear, she knows me. She makes an effort to talk and smile and be friendly. This is not a stranger. I tell Amber this as we saunter into the dress store expecting a warm welcome. I see the store owner, who I have seen one billion times before, and say, "Hello, how are you?" This woman just stares, does not say a word. I can tell by the look on her face that she has no earthly idea who I am. Me being taken out of my familiar surroundings has made me a stranger. Also, her rudeness is something store owners do when they don't want you in their store. I quickly turn to Amber and tell her, "This woman has no idea who I am. I see her all the time, but she can't recognize me outside of the store." We laugh our butts off. This is going to be hilarious. We start looking at the dresses and the owner is just staring at us. You can tell she thinks we are in the wrong store and finally she makes her way over to us. I speak first and say my sister is getting married so we are looking for dresses. I'm thinking now that this fool is closer, maybe she will recognize me or even my voice. Nope, nothing. Instead this woman says, "I don't sell wedding dresses." Now, I know what you're thinking: why didn't we just leave? At this point I just wanted her to have to be in the same space as the two Black women she couldn't wait to get out of her store. I also wanted to report to the other store owners about my treatment when I visited her store. I tell her any dress can be a wedding dress, my sister is a nontraditional bride and is just looking for a nice evening dress. Her face twists up and she says, "Really? I still don't think I have anything." We keep looking around. Frustrated, she finally blurts out, "You know getting married is overrated these days. Is that what you really want?" She really said this. This woman wanted us to leave her store so badly that instead of getting a commission on a dress, she tried to get Amber to call off her wedding!

Also, why did she say "getting married is overrated"? Did she expect us to be all like, *Wow, thank you for saying that, my eyes have been opened. Never mind! Let me cancel the cake; let me send a million emails; let me talk to my in-laws; let me call the venue and tell them to shove it; let me glue the confetti back into full sheets of paper; let me deflate all these balloons; let me call my fiancé and cancel the wedding because this foolish old harpy told me weddings were overrated. Thank you, thank you for saving me!*

We walk around the store a little bit longer making her feel very uncomfortable. Being sure to try to touch everything in sight as she watches. We finally leave, and when we step just outside her store, we talk to each other about how rude this old woman was and if we had been white women this never would have happened. We make sure she can hear our whole conversation. This woman is unfazed. The next time I'm at work she stops by, ready to yap like best friends do. She has no idea I was the lady in the store. This idiot. I tell her how it was my sister and I who stopped by her store the other day and she was very rude, especially telling my sister that getting married was overrated. I can see the color drain from her face, and she leaves the store. I walk around the mall that day and let a few store owners know about her behavior. None are surprised.

Oooh! That reminds me of the time we were in Paris and the mean store clerk.

Oh, you mean the time in Paris when you made us late to the airport and we missed our flight back to the US?

Shut up, Lacey. Let me tell our story.

WORST PARIS EXPERIENCE

Lacey and I were having the time of our lives in Paris. We went to restaurants and clothing stores and in and out of neighborhoods. Now, word on the street is, Paris is quite racist. I mean they tried to outlaw hijabs at one point, sooooo not as far as I can throw 'em. Josephine Baker being in the pantheon means nothing. Nice try, Paris.
So, as we began to explore, we encounter your normal Paris rudeness, frustration with our being tourists and our poor French skills—

My French was great, speak for yourself.

I speak for both of us when I say we stink.
We decide to go shopping. We noticed that some storekeepers were standing at the doorway welcoming you in, but some storekeepers were standing in the doorway to stop you

from coming in. That was something I had never seen before. Now, you might think being in Paris is a wonderful experience, but you're gonna encounter some pretty high-level racism. A special racism that stems from snobbery. Classist AND racist. Racism connoisseurs like ourselves appreciate it.

So we find a store with no one in the doorway and think, *Oh, we are in luck! We can just walk right in!* There's a lady behind the counter. She could not give one poop that we are in her store. After spending quite a bit of time in this clothing store, trying on clothes, and laughing and having the good time we always do, we are ready to check out. Each of us has an armful of clothes. We couldn't see any other customers in the store. It's just me and Lacey having fun. We walk up to the counter and put our stuff down. The woman stands there and pays us no mind. A white customer comes up to the counter right next to us and the woman rings her up, turns her back on us, and returns to what she was doing. We fucking left.

The worst doctor story has to be Lacey's dentist story. I hate it so bad that I can't tell it. Lacey has to.

WORST DENTIST

Oh my god, the dentist story. You guys. This is an insane one. If you google "Black people don't feel pain" you will find a plethora of stories and studies of the trauma we've had to endure when visiting the doctor. Not to mention the blatant disrespect we get from everyone at the offices, including the receptionists. Not saying it happens at every visit for every person of color, but it happens enough that there are documented studies and real stories from people of color proving this happens way too often. Please see the kidney stone story from the first book. Okay, so I end up seeing an orthodontist all the way out in Bellevue. At the time, I lived there to be closer to work. You never want to go too deep into a white neighborhood to be seen by a doctor because you don't want to be anyone's first Black patient. It's not a guarantee, but usually doctors in a more mixed neighborhood will do great things like listen to you and make eye contact. But it's always a gamble. This time, I chose convenience over the golden rule. I was young and the concept of getting an "in-neighborhood" doctor was just something old people say at this point. I had no proof. I was about to get proof.

So, the orthodontist tells me I'm going to need four teeth pulled. That's fine. I have never been scared of dental work. I would have to go to his partner, a dentist, to get it done. I get there and the receptionist is disgusted to see me. She's rude as all get-out. But, how bad can they be? The orthodontist upstairs is fine. This is just the receptionist. She's probably got her own set of problems.

The door to the rest of the office opens. The dentist calls me in. He doesn't seem terribly racist at first glance. Real normal looking. I go up and follow him back to the room. He's not too nice, and he's not too mean. He just seems like he's done this a thousand times and is just going through the motions. He gets the Novocain and shoots my mouth full of it. He puts it in the four different places where he's planning on pulling the four different teeth. After I'm all numb he gets to work. He's pulling, pulling. Nothing is happening. He's pulling, pulling, pulling some more on each of the four teeth, and nothing budges. He goes to get something that looks like an ice pick. Not very scary to me, but I'm all numbed up. Have at it. Boy, does he. He is digging and digging. Nothing budges. He digs and digs and digs some more on each tooth, and it's nothing. Then, he resorts to something dentists have heard of but have never seen in real life. This man lowers my chair and straddles me. It is as if I were a wild bull, and he's trying to hold on for seven seconds. Only I am perfectly still and it lasts a lot longer than that. He yanks and yanks at all four teeth with all his might while, and I can't stress this enough, straddling me. It was like a lap dance went as bad as it could go.

He gives up. They're not budging. Defeated, he dismounts me. He just can't pull 'em out. He's got a red face and is out of breath. He was unable to pull out a single tooth. "We're gonna have to send you to an oral surgeon. They're impacted." Now, although I'm all numbed up, this will only last a little while. I say to him, "I have to go out like this? Isn't this gonna be horrible? Aren't I gonna be in pain?" He says, "Yep. The receptionist will take care of you." And just like that, he leaves.

I assume they're going to call a special, nearby oral surgeon, and I can just hurry right over there. I go out to the receptionist who is even more disgusted to have to deal with me a second time. Everyone is looking at me like I'm crazy. This rude receptionist calls two people. No one can get me in that day. It's starting to sink in. This man has torn my mouth to shreds and just sent me out into the world to die. I get loud: "No, no, no, no. I need someone NOW. Find someone now." The receptionist is livid, and I'm crying. Not because I can feel anything but because I know I'm about to be in some unimaginable pain. This lady is moving as slow as molasses, while taking special care to keep giving me the stink eye. This office was disgusted to have me. They tore my mouth apart and discarded me like garbage. I have to take care of this myself. She tells me the soonest someone can get me in is in three days. Three days. I leave with absolutely nothing, no pain meds, not even a lollipop.

I drive home as fast as I can, search for the phone book, and call the first oral surgeon I find. A receptionist picks up. Not even the surgeon, the receptionist. I tell her what has happened and she screams, "What? Get here now! We will take care of you! Just get here as fast as you can!" It's gonna be a twenty-five-minute drive. I drop the phone and run to the bathroom. As I leave, I just so happen to see my face out of the corner of my eye. There is blood from my nose to my boobs. Just a solid square of blood like I'm a vampire and I just drank a whole person. So with all the staff at the dentist office no one told me I was covered in blood? No one cared to hand me a napkin or a wet wipe or send me out of their establishment with a shred of dignity? I've never in my life wished I were a white woman, but that day had me pretty close. Imagine if this had happened to a white woman. They would have tripped all over themselves to make sure she was pristine when she left.

I've gone up to strangers to inform them they had a piece of lint on their shirt, and no one in the whole office, patients included, could tell you you looked like Carrie on the stage at prom drenched in pigs' blood?

I guess not. Anyway, I clean up the best I can and rush out the door.

On the drive there, I start feeling it. Ten minutes in and I'm wondering if I'm gonna make it. I get to the office and a team of people are waiting for me. They rush me back and the dentist goes, "I can numb these or I can just pull 'em." I say, "I don't know." Because honestly, I don't. I don't even know where I am at this point. They decide to try Novocain for the first one. He put the needle in and, like a rocket, I shoot up out of the chair. The assistant pushes me back down. I ask, "What was that?" The assistant goes, "Did it feel like someone was electrocuting you?" I tell her it did. She says, "We must have hit a nerve."

"Just pull 'em."

The dentist pulls four frigging teeth without Novocain while I scream at the top of my lungs. Afterward, the dentist said, "These were the easiest teeth to pull." "They weren't impacted?" I ask. "Nope. They shouldn't have sent you away. And, if they had to, they should have given you pain meds."

I looked into lawyers but no one wanted to take my case. I wonderrrrr whyyyyy.

MOST RACIST FUNDRAISERS

And sometimes, white people don't believe that there's a double standard.

While I was working at a retirement home in a small town right outside of Omaha, my job asked me to do the unimaginable. I had worked at places that were struggling financially before, but this one was unique. They were running out of money so badly that, and I'm not kidding, they started a GoFundMe so they could pay the bills. Now, I don't know if you want your grandma living at a retirement home that relies on a GoFundMe, but I do not. On my first day my boss catches me up pretty quick on the financial situation. She tells me that the business has fallen on financial hardship, and the previous program director was planning a garage sale that weekend to raise money for the building. And my first project as program director would be to pick up where she left off. I was told lots of staff are signed up for the home's garage sale because they loved the last program director so much. All I would need to do is go around and confirm who is coming. She also told me both maintenance workers will be there because there are some very heavy pieces of furniture upstairs for sale and they would be able to help me move them.

So, I leave her office to verify my list of helpers on my first day.

Fun fact: When you are a person of color and you start a job at a place where there are no other minorities you will immediately get a feel for whether or not you're welcome. I WAS NOT. As I went around to everyone, I was hit with such comments as, "*You're* the new program director?!" "Wow, we are really going to miss Cheryl, she was great." And "I miss Cheryl. I wish she was still running this garage sale." Looks like I had some big shoes to fill. So I asked one of the residents how long Cheryl had worked there and was told she quit after three damn months. Three months? Three months of working with this woman has you gazing off into the distance pining for her return? Hmmm. Sounds suspicious. Also, there are several certified nursing assistants and nurses who are just plain mean mugging me and whispering like it's junior high. What in the world have I gotten myself into? So, as I'm asking everyone about the garage sale, I notice a trend. Everyone who had previously signed up for it was suddenly unable to go. Every last one of them. Some of them give me very creative excuses but most say they never signed up or that they don't remember signing up at all. Hmmm. Doing you dirty by signing you up for this weekend activity without your permission? Doesn't sound like your hero Cheryl to me. Sounds to me like this entire place was giving me the cold shoulder for fun.

Now, even though I'm pissed, I don't beg them or get upset or even raise my voice. I first go back to my office and call my mother. I just need to vent. She gets mad right along with me and asks, "Well, are you still going to do it?" I tell her I'm not sure; I need to speak with the boss. I go back to my boss's office and tell her no one is going to show up this weekend. She truly does not seem surprised. She tried to reassure me by saying that she and another director will be there and the three of us will just have to do our best. I say okay, and keep planning the garage sale with the three of us for the rest of the week. It's an odd situation to be in but at least I'm not in it alone! So, the day of the garage sale comes and guess what? The two directors didn't show up. It was what I feared. I was left to take care of this whole bad idea and it wasn't going to be easy. Neighborhood flyers had been sent out all over town and they even ran a damn ad in the local newspaper. To make matters worse, the director had the nerve to message me and tell me to bring down the furniture from upstairs. She said maintenance had left me a dolly and she was sure I was strong enough to move it. So, I went up there with the dolly and put all the furniture...I'm just kidding. I left that shit upstairs. Needless to say, this was not the garage sale they had hoped for. I came back to work on Monday and my director apologized profusely about not being able to make it. Meanwhile, I'm already on Indeed looking for my next disaster.

A week or so later, the boss calls me into her office with another idea to raise money for the building. She wants me, Lacey Lamar, beautiful brown-skinned Lacey, to go around this white town and ask people to donate money to the retirement home. She wants me, a Black woman, to walk into businesses in this small town—the same town of racist doughnuts,* which is bad enough, but also ask them for MONEY. Me, the only Black person here, to run around panhandling. She told me the folks around here are very friendly and shouldn't hesitate to donate. I ask her, "Are they as friendly as your staff, because I did not get a friendly welcome from them." I also let her know as a Black woman, I will not be walking around this town asking for money. I did not think this was a good idea. She stares at me, truly trying to comprehend what I'm saying, and says, "I really don't understand what you mean, but if you are uncomfortable I'm sure I can find someone else." Now, this may seem a bit extreme, but this is not my first small town, and I know exactly what's gonna happen if I start running in and out of stores here. I go back to my office and later that day my coworker Debbie comes by my office and says she has drafted this great letter asking businesses to donate to the building. She wants to take me out to lunch and stop at a couple of places to drop the letters off. I tell her lunch sounds great but I won't have anything to do with asking for money. She says that's fine. I could just wait in the car. Before we go to lunch she says she's going to drop the letter off at this little boutique she goes to all the time. As we pull up I notice a really cute dress in the window. Oh lord. Maybe it won't be bad because I'm with a white person. I decided to build up the strength to go in with her. We both walk in at the same time, so the cashier knows we're together. The white woman

---

* Racist doughnuts is from the first book. It's maybe my favorite story of all time.

working there can't stop staring at me. I smile and say hello. She says nothing. Debbie immediately goes into her spiel about how she is trying to raise money for the retirement home and hands her the letter. The woman does not look at the letter but looks Debbie straight in the eye and says, "Why is SHE here?" I look at Debbie and say "See? This is why I didn't want to do this." And I leave the store. Debbie follows me out, saying, "Okay, that was a little weird. I don't know why she said that!" I say "I do and I won't be going with you to any more businesses to ask for money." She ends up mailing the letters.

LARGEST BLIND SPOT

While working at a girls' and boys' group home in Omaha I came to work one day and began to share with two coworkers a documentary I had watched the night before. These two guys were my favorite staff to work with. They were very down-to-earth, lovable, and easy to talk to. So as you can imagine I was completely shocked when they started mocking me about watching this show. The documentary was about the civil war in Rwanda, the genocide. I shared how hundreds of thousands of people were murdered. I shared how the documentary focused on one young boy and how hard his life was since being turned into a child soldier. I'm almost in tears when I finish telling them about the documentary. They are in complete denial. They are asking questions like, "Wait, a war? A real war? Wouldn't we have seen this on TV? Wars just don't happen without everyone knowing about them." Then these idiots say, "Oh and they are using children? That makes no sense." When I try to explain to them about genocide, one of them says, "A race war? In Africa? They are all the same race. That makes no sense. Listen to yourself. Why did you watch this?" So they go on and on and are actually laughing. Laughing at what I just told them. I try to explain to them that this is actually real, but it doesn't matter what I say, they are calling it a "fake war." So after that every time I come into work and see them, they say things like, "Hey, Lacey, how's that fake war going?" "Heard anything else about the race war? Pots versus kettles?" Dang. That last one was good, but I have to go to their supervisor and sadly explain to them how this is inappropriate and they need to cool it. They're given a stern talking-to. And after a while, they stop. But it's too late. My hate for them grew too strong! I understand having a blind spot. I understand not knowing what's going on in the world, but these guys had a blind spot the size of Africa. Which I assume they assume is a country.

CHAPTER SIX

CHRYSTAL'S IN THE MIX!

G race. Dignity. Passion. When I think of those words, I
think of myself, but let's talk about Chrystal. Chrystal is
our oldest sister who, all jokes aside, is a pretty cool cucumber. The thing about her is she's lived all over. She's lived in
Panama, Wyoming, Hawaii. She's seen the best and the
worst! So, she's got as good a Spidey sense as anyone else.
The thing about Chrystal is, she loves people. She has the
ability to see the good in them, and that's why I think she's a
forgiving person. I'd call her the most forgiving of us all. She's
almost as calm as Dad. I can't imagine anyone getting her
riled up. She's too smart and too chill. Here's proof: During
the following stories, Chrystal kills exactly zero people. Keep
count!

MOST RACIST SCHOOL

Chrystal moved to Sydney, Australia. Just kidding. Sydney,
Nebraska! So, she moves to this small town in about 1998

and is registering her kids for the school year. The town is completely white and Chrystal is aware of what she's about to get into. Look, we all know it's not gonna be the best, but she's hoping that maybe it won't be hilarious. And, I'm sorry to report that that is not the case.

So, Chrystal gets to the school and goes to the office to register the kids. She can immediately tell by the way it feels when she walks in that she is in for it. It's how everyone stops what they're doing to look at her. It's how silent they get. It's how the woman behind the counter greets her. And—this is controversial and I'm sorry—the woman has a racist accent. I know, I know, accents can't be racist, but I gotta go with life experience on this one. Also, maybe you'll hear what I mean by the end of the story.

Okay so, Chrystal sees what she's up against and employs her only defense—extreme kindness.

> *Chrystal:* Hi, there! How are you?
> *Seemingly Nice Woman:* Oh, I'm all right. How can I help you?
> *Chrystal:* I'm new to town, and I'd like to register my children for the school year, please.
> *The "Uh-oh I've Heard Her Accent and Now I Know" Woman:* Great! Well, welcome! All you need to do is fill out this and this.
> *Chrystal:* Okay.
> *The Queen of Oh No Elementary:* And this and this...

Chrystal: Will do.

That Lady She Can Already See a Bad Future With: And we'll need a picture of the children.

Chrystal: What?

She Who We Legally Can't Name: We're gonna take a picture of your children and pass it around school and show it to all the students so they don't get scared.

Chrystal: ...

No One's Favorite: But it should be all right. We've had Nigra children here before.

Ohhhhkay and that's where the accent comes in. For those of you reading this book, the lady was trying to say "Negro." But for those of you listening to the audiobook, you know damn well what we're talking about. But, see what I mean? That's that racist accent. It's not Southern, 'cause that would be "Neeegra." It's specifically Midwest racist. It's "Nigra." It's bad!

So, the rest of the story is, Chrystal is shook. She's only got one choice. She's gotta make with the pictures and fast. 'Cause if these people need to see Black people in order to not feel scared, then there's no telling what the fuck these little monsters are capable of. She shows them the pictures, and the kids have as bad a time as you'd expect.

MOST RACIST BANK

When Chrystal was in high school she worked at a McDonald's. But not one in North Omaha, where there are other Black people, one in West Omaha, where there are significantly fewer Black people. This was all the way out on 132nd and Maple. Which may be more diverse now, but at this time is very white. So, in order to cash her check, she had to walk down to 120th and Maple to some bank we forget the name of. She'd walk down there every other week to cash her check. The people there knew her and were nice! It was a regular, friendly place. Well, one cold September day, Chrystal strolled in there like usual and the second she stepped in the door, the security guard was in her face. This wasn't the normal guy she was used to seeing, this was a newer, more insane person. This security guard approached her and loudly and angrily was like, "You have to take off your gloves." Chrystal looked down and saw he had his hand on his gun. A teenage girl whose face you can completely see enters a bank and this genius is like, "Take off your gloves...so that I can see if you have a manicure or not?...'cause I have a hand fetish?...in case of high fives?" Guys, I cannot make that one make sense. Let's break it down:

So, does he think she's a robber and is trying to get her to leave fingerprints everywhere? And that her fingerprints would be better than his full description of her baby face?[*] If

---

[*] When you read that, did you also think of Kenneth "Babyface" Edmonds? If so, please text Lacey "Amber loves Babyface more than you." She's gonna be so mad.

102

he thought she was a robber, didn't he just make it easier for Chrystal to wield her gun? He ought to know, 'cause HIS HAND IS ON HIS GUN AS HE'S TALKING TO THIS CHILD. Make it make sense, Lord. And, has anyone, anywhere ever been asked to take off their gloves when entering any place? Like, is there a scenario in which it could make the teeniest bit of sense? If you've figured out an answer, please write it down and eat it.

So, Chrystal is shook. She's young and scared and face-to-face with this super angry guy who I'm guessing lives to scare children. She rips off her gloves and can feel panic setting in. (Something I hope you'll never have to deal with is an irate person yelling orders at you while subtly, I guess not-so-subtly, threatening your life. Like, why isn't it just "Do what I say?" Why does it have to be "Do what I say or I'll shoot you?") Anyway, Chrystal is feeling scared because this man is angry for a reason she can't nail down and is asking her to do things that make no sense. As she's about to start crying, her regular bank teller yells over "Chrystal, are you ready?" The security guard looks behind him and Chrystal zips right over to her. Maybe the teller knew the guard was scaring her. Maybe she wanted to hurry up and go on break. We don't know. What we do know is—fuck that guy.

SNITCHING-EST NEIGHBOR

So, not too long ago, Chrystal used to live in North Platte, a small city in Nebraska. July 4, 2019, and here is a good place to stop and say, this woman is the only person in our family who can remember a date.

Two days after our third anniversary, my husband and I turned to each other and said, "Wait. Did we miss our anniversary?" We laughed ourselves to bits and have forgotten it more times than we've remembered it. Probably five out of eleven years.

Oh my God, can **one** thing not be about you without you losing your dang mind?

I'm sorry I keep talking about mememememememmeme.

And now I'm being informed that my shutting up is integral to my health. Let's continue.

July 4, 2019. Chrystal's in a Walmart and her phone rings. She answers it because it is a North Platte number. It could be work; it could be a client. You never know. But she picks up and it's Officer So-and-so! Some North Platte police officer. They're calling for an unbelievable reason. Now, people always talk about how white folks think the police are at their beck and call 24-7. I always thought that was more of an exaggeration, but MAAAAAAN! This cop called Chrystal because one of her neighbors said she speeds through the neighborhood and has to slow down. That is the reason the police called. Because they heard from a person that Chrystal may be driving too fast—something they do not know and cannot prove. A rumor about a Black lady's driving habits warranted a phone call! Guys. Needless to say, that neighbor did not have a radar gun or any way to know how fast Chrystal was driving. And if you've ever ridden with Chrystal, she is not the speediest person.

She's not. In fact, here's every Ruffin driver in order of speed from slowest to fastest:

Dad
Angie
Chrystal
Amber
Lacey
Mom
Jimmy

And Jimmy's not exactly whipping through town either, but as far as Ruffins go, he's pretty fast, making Chrystal pretty dang slow.

Now, this isn't Chrystal's first white town. She always sets her cruise control so that she knows she's going the speed limit. So, she knows this is more about her driving around the neighborhood than her driving too fast. She's sure the cops just wanted her to know that they're keeping an eye on her. Look, it's the Fourth of July, Chrystal has to get over to Mom and Dad's 'cause she's got volleyball to win. She isn't fazed. She's very nice to the police officer even though he's a bitch. She lives in that neighborhood for a while and never gets a speeding ticket. Her neighbors are sorely disappointed.

MOST RACIST EASTER

One Easter, a million years ago, Angie and Chrystal dressed OUT. If you love the eighties, you would have loved it. They were wearing polka dots and peplum shirts over pencil skirts. They had matching outfits, matching belts, matching Jheri curls, and matching purses with brand-new little spray bottles of Jheri curl juice in them. Anyways, on this very special day, Angie and Chrystal were really feeling themselves, and for good reason. These two wanted to make the most of these outfits, so they decided to walk to the store and get the big bottle of Jheri curl juice that they had run out of. I mean, those purse-sized ones were fine, but we needed some for the *household*. So, they get to Walgreens, toot around, and find what they're looking for: a big ol' bottle of activator.

Hi, white people. "Activator" is Jheri curl juice.

Hi, other white people, yes, we are spelling it correctly. The Jheri curl is a permanent wave hairstyle that was popular among Black people during the eighties. It was invented by a hairstylist named Jheri Redding.

Now, Chrystal and Angie, at this point, had spent a lot of time in the store. With outfits that bad, they had to be seen. But the cashier sees their little bottles of product when they open up their purses to pay for the big bottle. They call security. Security comes over, checks their purses, and finds their travel-sized Jheri curl juice! The bottles were brand-new and were sold at that Walgreens so, when they find these bottles, they assume they were stolen and fucking take them! Now, I know people are always stealing from Walgreens but in this case, Walgreens stole from them! Chrystal and Angie went home and told Mom. But it was too late. Mom threw away the receipt and there was nothing they could do. Their Jheri curls both dried up and blew away. Just kidding. Wait. I'm only kind of just kidding 'cause listen to this— Sorry. If you're reading, you can't listen to this. Wait. Yes, you can. Read this next part out loud.

So, we all went to a middle school called Nathan Hale. I called it Nathan Hell because I was a really cool guy. So, at Nathan Hale, you had to take swim classes. But, because Chrystal had a Jheri curl, her hair would never snap back after she had to swim. The chlorine would react with the activator, and it would result in bald patches. So, she talks to the teacher. The teacher says, "You can sit out of swimming if you get a doctor's note." Chrystal goes to the doctor, shows him her bald patches, and the doctor says, "That's the way their hair is supposed to look." That doctor thought that Black people just naturally had bald spots? Or, and this is more likely, the doctor didn't want Chrystal to get out of having to swim. Who the fuck thinks, *Welp, here we are in this landlocked state. Better make it a requirement for kids to learn how to swim at this school and this school alone!* So, Chrystal kept having to take swim class and her hair kept falling out. Look, we don't have a lot of happy endings around here. She looks fine now. Fun fact: She already knew how to swim because my parents made us all take classes when we were children. The only one who doesn't know how to swim is me, and it's a very fun story so indulge me:

So, I'm five years old. It's time to take swim lessons! Dad

takes me every week and watches from the bleachers and every week I have more fun than the last. We get in the shallow end and splash around and laugh and laugh! The teacher is so nice and he looks just like Tom Selleck. I'm friends with each and every kid in there and we are all in love. (At least, this is how I remember it.) So, every week, at the end of class, the teacher has us put our heads under water. And it is at this point, every week, I lose my shit. When the teacher tries to convince me that this is an okay thing to do, I just flip the fuck out. I've never acted this way before and probably haven't since but the thought of putting my head under water is terrifying. Welp, this is extremely embarrassing and difficult to understand for my dad. He is part dolphin and is a very good swimmer. And he's had enough of my horseshit. One week, I'm all ready to go to swim class and he looks me in the eye and goes, "You had better put your head under water this week, or you're gonna get a spanking." Now, these were different times, blah, blah, blah, but also, in order to get a spanking in our house, you had to really want it. I can remember only two spankings—when Jimmy set the garage on fire and when we stayed out waaaaay past when the streetlights came on. Two in my entire life. So when Dad threatens a spanking, I know he means business.

So we get to class and are having a ball. It may be the funnest class yet. I am just built for the water! I'm a sweet little water baby just like Dad! And then it happens. It is time to put our heads under water. Now, I have two options: Get a spanking or drown the instant my head submerges in the water. I lose my mind. I start screaming, "I want a spanking!

I want a spanking!" Mind you, no one knows why I am doing this. They just thought I went extra crazy this week. "I want a spaaaankiiing!!!" Dad calmly walks down from the bleachers, plucks me out of the water, tucks me under his arm, and takes me home. I do not get a spanking and never learn how to swim.

But this isn't about me, it's about Chrystal! Now almost every Black person our age remembers learning this in school at one point or another. And this isn't a superlative but, Chrystal's "slavery wasn't bad" story is this: It was somewhere in elementary school, her teacher told the class that "People try to make a big deal about it but slavery wasn't that bad." The teacher's logic was, "At least enslaved people had food to eat. The Russians were cold and naked! Isn't that a lot worse than being enslaved?" Bitch, they were free!

I know! I swear, the same people who lose their mind about their right to have a gun in a daycare are the same people who think slavery wasn't that bad. It's like, you can't even obey basic laws! Do you think you could be forced to work in captivity for someone for free till you die from it and be like, "Welp, that sure is some good eatin'!" I think the fuck not.

MOST RACIST PILOT

When they were young, Chrystal and Angie took aviation classes. And it's at this point I realize I forgot to say, Mom and Dad put us in all kinds of classes. Learning new stuff was always encouraged. You were allowed to take whatever weird classes you wanted. Or if there was a special summer school program you wanted to be a part of, you could! Ruffins love to take classes about things they know nothing about. Awww man, I wish I had a picture of when we all took a belly dancing class. That was the best time I've ever had while being the absolute worst I've ever been at anything. So, Angie and Chrystal are in this aviation class and it's them and a bunch of little white boys. The teacher, a pilot, comes hot out the gate with: "Piloting is not for everyone. There are plenty of careers you have to choose from." Then, this piece of shit looks right at Chrystal and Angie and says, "Some people are more cut out for departments like housekeeping." They went right home and told Mom. And you best believe that after a stern talking-to, this man figured out how to act right. Chrystal and Angie are now pilots for Delta Airlines. Just kidding.

But that talking-to did fix his attitude problem right then and there! And not to put too fine a point on it, but why would you say this to children? Are you scared that the little white boys would feel equal to the little Black girls? Or were you just getting off on being mean to little Black children? Or, and this is the true one: BOTH.

MOST RACIST EMPLOYEE GANG

Just a little bit ago in Lincoln, Nebraska, Chrystal goes to the mall with two young sweeties: her daughter and her daughter's friend. So, they park outside of Dillard's and walk through it to get into the rest of the mall. As they're coming out of Dillard's, there's a security guard right there at the exit. He starts talking into his shoulder walkie-talkie thing and Chrystal is like, "Awww dang, they're about to get someone now!" The way he was frantically yelling into that thing made them sure he had just caught people doing some bad shit! Odd that he was making eye contact with Chrystal when he was doing it but who knows? So, the three of them shop in the mall for a bit and on the way out, they go through Dillard's again. This time making a stop in purses and shoes. On their way in, they catch a security guard. He follows them. Nothing new about that. He finds a nice place to hang as he watches them from afar. They're looking at this and that when a woman comes over. "Hi! Can I help you with anything?" "Nope. Just looking." The woman stands a few feet away and watches them. Not even a full minute goes by until another person comes over. "Hello. Can I help you with anything?" "Nope. We are just looking, thank you." Now, that person stands a few feet away, too. Within two minutes they've got three people staring them down. Four. Five. They keep looking around. Six people. Then, Chrystal's daughter finds a purse she thinks is cute. They all laugh about the fact that it costs $987. She picks it up, and they all look at it. At this point, Chrystal looks around and realizes they've mobilized the entire staff. It was bad enough before, but now they're touching something that costs a thousand dollars, and that's not gonna fly. People were right in their faces on all sides; it was like the employees were standing in a circle. It felt like they were blocking them from making a run for it. Now, they couldn't say out loud, "Get out of this store right now!" But they could certainly send that vibe. And vibe received! It was like they were in a bubble of hate. Chrystal puts the purse down and escorts the children out of the mall. The horde of people follows them for a while. They get to the car and can breathe easier. Even the kids knew what was up. That made Chrystal sad but what better place to learn about racism than Dillard's! Chrystal is not petty, but she regrets not buying that purse to this day.

MOST RACIST HOA

Years ago, Chrystal moved into a house in Denton, Nebraska, that had a homeowners association. It was in an all-white neighborhood, so watch out. She considered not going to the HOA meeting. But then she realized that wasn't really an option. You see, if she didn't go then she could have easily been the subject of the meeting where they all agreed to have her surveilled or god knows what. So she decides to go. As she drives into town, she grows more and more scared. She sees sketchy bars, Republican campaign signs, and too many American flags and knows exactly where she is. Gulp. She walks in and almost walks right back out. The whole place is staring her down and if looks could kill, she would have died. But, it's too late to turn back now. She sits down, and immediately a lady taps her on the shoulder, looks her in the eye, and says, "You're not supposed to be here." And, you coulda heard a pin drop. Everyone is staring at Chrystal, who silently looks at this lady. The woman catches herself and says, "I'm sorry. I mean, are you here for the HOA meeting?" Chrystal smiles and says yes. The woman felt so bad that she sat next to Chrystal and talked to her for the whole meeting. But she should not have felt bad. She shoulda felt great because she helped Chrystal prepare to live in yet another neighborhood that sucked a butt.

LEAST FUN RACIST

Years ago, Chrystal worked at a youth detention center. She was in training to be a supervisor. Which was great but before she got this job she had twenty years of experience in this field so it was a step back. On her tour of the facilities she's being led around and gets shown the male unit. As they walk through Chrystal can see a young man pacing in his room through a window on his door. He's pacing and yelling and cursing up a storm. You'd think someone was in there with him by the way he was yelling. All of a sudden, he snaps out of it. He jumps to the window on his door and yells to Chrystal, "Oh my god! A Black female worker! Congratulations, lady!" That shoulda told her how bad it was gonna be. This man was so shocked to see a Black woman there that it snapped him out of what very well may have been a psychotic episode.

This is the part of the book where I do my best to stay on topic instead of exploring mental illness and the American justice system.

At this facility, Chrystal's coworkers were a little sad they had to work the overnight Christmas shift. So, to make it fun, Chrystal stopped by the dollar store and bought some silly presents and organized a bingo game with everyone on staff. They had such a good time that word got out, and Chrystal organized games with all the other shifts so that everyone could have a chance to play. This infuriated her bosses. She got called into the office. The warden said: "It's unfair to have special events for just one shift."

> **Chrystal:** I know. That's why we have scheduled the same thing with every other shift.
> **Warden G:** Well, someone could bring a lawsuit against you for this.
> **Chrystal:** What in the world could I possibly be sued for? That makes no sense.
> **Bore-den:** You can't just give away free stuff.
> **Chrystal:** ...
> **Warden Beatty:** Cancel it.

(I'll give you a million dollars if you successfully understood that last warden pun.) And she canceled it. And everyone continues to do their jobs just a little bit sadder.

When Chrystal first started at the youth detention center she got in trouble for taking one of the inmates through a stretch of hallway that has no camera coverage. Her supervisor brought her in and pointed this out and reprimanded her and gave her a write-up. That hallway is the only hallway the inmates can take to get outside. Each inmate goes outside once a day. Everyone does this. There is no other way to do this. He wrote her up for fun.

Chrystal quickly became the person who had to speak up on behalf of minorities for minority stuff. Like when there was a Black girl who came in wearing a wig. They immediately wanted her to take it off. They didn't want her to wear it, but it wasn't big, it was a tiny pixie Halle Berry wig. There was not a weapon that could fit in it. Chrystal explained that "A wig is not a shirt or a pair of socks, this is cultural. And most importantly, completely within the rules for her to have here. She has rights. This is not jail." The girl got special permission. Chrystal enjoyed the tiny win. It would be the last win against racism she would have! KIDDING! (Mostly.)

DUDE. I did not intend for this to be *The Ruffin Book of Music* but, here we are. I just remembered something fun. This is a song Chrystal and Angie used to sing that I frigging adored.

♪♪I'm the fireman, I'm ready to go, I'm the fireman!
I'm the fireman and I'm ready to go
Bright red hat and a rubber hose
Putting out fires in yo crib
I never got a medal for what I did
I'm the fireman, I'm ready to go, I'm the fireman!♪♪

And just for fun, here's the cutest picture you've ever laid eyes on!

CHAPTER SEVEN

MOST WHITE PRIVILEGE

H ere are some unbelievable stories of white privilege. During this next section of white privilege at its best, let's play a game called Can Black People Do This? If there are any Black people who have done any of these stories and have kept their jobs, or stayed out of jail, Lacey Lamar will give you a $1 billion check.*

"YOU PEED A LITTLE ON THE TOILET SEAT"

This is at the same job where I received a Black doll as a bribe to not leave. (Please see our first book if you are not familiar with that story.) Also, I was the only person of color who worked there. I worked there alongside an older woman named Chrissy. Now, what you are about to read about Chrissy no person of color could ever get away

---

* Meaning I will "check" and see if you have $1 billion. If you do, I'll take it.

with doing at their job. Chrissy is completely clueless and otherwise harmless. Honestly, she's not even the one at this job saying racist things. She's just a bit of TMI mixed with wide-eyed honesty. I would not say she was racist, but she does an excellent job of showing you how white privilege works. One day, the CEO and his wife were flying in and wanted to meet the director's team at the morning meeting. This had never happened before and was understood to be a big deal. Our boss does not want to be embarrassed. We all meet them at the door, shake hands, everyone is on their best behavior. Before the meeting started, we all grabbed a water or coffee, finished up whatever was on our computers, used the bathroom, and went to the conference room. As we file in, my coworker Chrissy walks over to the CEO's wife and lowers her voice, but not low enough so that everyone in the room can't hear her, and she says in a sweet, singsongy tone something that needs its own space,

"You know, I went into the restroom right after you, and you peed a little on the toilet seat."

Maybe I exaggerate a lot or maybe no one has ever said anything this funny in the history of the world. This woman walked up to the CEO's rich-ass wife and said, "You peed a little on the toilet seat." Everything went silent and I could hear my own heartbeat. It was the most tension I've ever felt. And I wasn't even the fool who said this. I was frozen along with everyone else in the room. The wife nervously lets out a short laugh and says, "What? No, I didn't." Now, if Chrissy had one drop of sense, she would have left this alone. But, reader, she has less sense than the toilet seat had pee! Chrissy immediately chimes back with even more confidence. "Yes, there was definitely three drops of pee on the seat." She said "three drops." Who counts the drops? Who comes back to a room full of people to report drops of pee on a toilet seat to their boss's boss? Who is this brave? Who is this bold? It is none other than Chrissy the mindless. "But don't worry" she says, squeezing the boss's wife's arm, "I cleaned it up." The wife recoils and walks away obviously disgusted, confused, and shocked by what had just happened. She stands next to her husband and the meeting begins but everyone remains mortified. Later, Chrissy is pulled aside by her boss and given a verbal reprimand. And you can bet that if I had decided to play pee pee police with my boss's boss, I would have been fired on the spot (of pee).

ANGRY PARNELL

Lacey is new at a residence and during the first morning meeting everyone seems like what you'd expect. Regular run-of-the-mill staff. So they go around talking about all the things they need to do or are planning to do and they bring up an issue with the head of maintenance. Let's call him Parnell. The boss says, "Parnell, there were four windows you were supposed to fix. You gonna get on that today?" This started a war. Parnell slams his fists on the table and starts yelling. The workload is too much for him. The boss tries to calm him down, but when Parnell starts cussing, all bets are off. The two of them have a shouting match the likes of which Lacey has never seen inside of a workplace. Parnell is verbally burning this place to the ground. Just full scorched earth. He must have some dynamite references 'cause after this display, he will need a new job. For the grand finale, Parnell storms out, shouting, "Fuck this place!" He leaves. Not the meeting. The building. He's gone. Lacey's shocked. She's never seen anything like this. What drama! Cool that she got to see a real-life *Fuck you, I quit!* It's just as fun as it is on TV. Once he's gone, everyone rolls their eyes and goes back to the meeting. No one is fazed. That's odd but who cares?

The next day, Lacey gets into the office and Parnell is there. Right back to work like he didn't cuss everybody all up one side and down the other. All right. Days go by and then at the morning meeting, the boss says, "Parnell, you were supposed to fix the flooring, why didn't you?" And, this man just plain loses it. And now, Lacey sees it. She didn't miss anything the first time. This man is just extremely volatile. Any little thing can and will set him off. He puts his full anger on display at his J-O-B, and no one gives a single rip.

A couple of days later: "Parnell, did you finish training your staff?" And this man turns into a giant baby and flips out. He leaves and comes back later that same day.

A few more days go by. "Parnell, did you fix the rolling beds?" Full nuclear meltdown.

Sometimes they would ask, "Did Parnell come back today?" Sometimes he did and sometimes he did not. This man could throw a temper tantrum and leave for days. And still come back to a J-O-B! Truly amazing. It was as if he was begging to get fired and never did. He was also just bad at his job. He got the whole building written up because he wouldn't do the work to make sure everything was up to code. That whole week the boss was like, "You have to fix this and this before the inspection." He did not and the company got fined $20,000. And that's when he finally got fired. JUST KIDDING HE STILL HAD A JOB AFTER THAT!! It was just common practice for him to jump up during the morning meetings, cuss a few people out, and leave. And then return to work whenever he felt like it. Must be nice. If Black people slam their fists on tables at work, jump up, and cuss people out we are escorted from the building by security.

COMING OUT OF THE CLOSET TWICE

At one of her jobs at a retirement home, Lacey had to work with a very wild and racist nurse. Let's call her Laura. Now, there was no way around working with this woman. Lacey describes Laura as what would happen if Blanche Deveraux from *The Golden Girls* and David Duke from the KKK had a baby. The thing about Laura is, she got caught having sex in the closet, in a retirement home with another employee. She then got fired. Got rehired, had more sex in the closet again, and kept her job. Now, I don't wanna sound lecherous but Laura is fine as hell and she knows it. I don't wanna sex shame her. Hey! If you wanna have sex in the closet at work, do it! Unless you're Black. Then, you will get fired. (I bet you thought that part was gonna be about how she was racist. Well, it's not. And it's not that she wasn't out-and-out racist quite a bit, it's just that compared to everyone else in this book, she can't compete.)

Once again, I'd like to say, if you are Black and have been caught twice having sex in a closet at work and you still have a job, please let me know. I need all the details!

ANIMAL HOUSE

So, it's Lacey's first day as a program director in this retirement home.

Sidenote: Please note how we aren't really connecting these workplaces to one another. At least, not as much as we could. That's because of plausible deniability. Like any place could be where one of these things happened but, if you can piece a bunch of these happenings together, you know exactly the place Lacey is talking about. The thing is, a lot of these people would get in trouble. And, we only sometimes want that to happen.

They're taking her around to every department, introducing her to people. And as they round the corner to a certain wing, Lacey immediately notices a smell. Not unusual in a retirement home but this one was special. A very special, very bad smell. The woman giving Lacey the tour notices Lacey notice the smell. As they approach the office, she turns to Lacey and says, "Listen. Don't say anything. We love this lady. Paula works hard and wears a hundred different hats but... you know... we have a little animal problem." They get into the office and Lacey sees that there are crates stacked up taller than she is and each crate has an animal in it. Lacey's guess is six or seven dogs. And the office is like a closet. Sorry, it *is* a closet. It's literally a closet they turned into an office. Now, Lacey loves animals. She has too many, in my opinion. So, if Lacey says you got too many animals, you got too many animals.

Excuse me? Two Great Danes, an African gray parrot, and a mallard duck are not too many animals, you coldhearted monster.

Anyway, this woman ran an animal rescue out of her office. She'd find strays or dogs that were gonna be put down and search for homes for them. And, here's the thing: she was great at it. As caring as she was good at finding homes for animals. Everyone loved her for a reason. Of course the lady whose heart is big enough to do this is very sweet. Sweet and lucky as hell to be white. Let Lacey work there for twenty years, lose her eyesight, and bring a seeing-eye dog in there and see how fast they throw her out.

Lacey is there for a few weeks and gets the hang of things. One day, Paula is out taking the residents on a leisurely drive. She loves to do it and the residents do, too. Lacey is at the office working. Someone runs up to her desk and says, "Lacey, we need your help. There's a dog loose in the build-ing." Now, sometimes the residents had little dogs of their own, so Lacey assumes it's one of those. She is very wrong. Paula had found a stray dog on their drive and put it in the van with the residents. A dog she did not know the history of. "Well, what kind of dog is it?" Lacey finds out it's a German shepherd and turns right back around. I need you to understand, at one of the most expensive retirement homes in Omaha a stray dog was accidentally let loose to run around. Does it bite? Does it have rabies? These are questions none of them have the answers to and Lacey wasn't going to find out. Some brave, foolish souls get together and put the dog back in the van until the Humane Society came.

If you are a person of color this is the last thing you would think of doing while on the job. Let me bring a potentially dangerous animal here and hope it goes well. Being white must make you very brave.

Some call it bravery, some call it lack of consequences.

WORK-LIFE IMBALANCE

When Lacey worked at a home for girls, there was a rule. You couldn't do three shifts in a row. But for some reason, this white man would do two shifts and then find an empty place to sleep. Whether it be a resident's spare room or the gym. And he'd stay there. As in, he would work, eat, go to bed, wake up, eat, and work, all while at work. Even though he had a home. He had started bringing his clothes to work, did laundry, he'd order extra dinners for the girls and eat them himself before going to sleep in a random office. I cannot stress enough that this man had a home. One day, someone flat-out said, "You know the man who lives here?" And Lacey was like "Lives here? A grown man should not be living at a girls' home." But it's okay that he was staying at work because he was homeless. That was a test to see if you've been paying attention. This man had a WHOLE ASS HOME but stayed close to pick up shifts. LET a Black man live in a girls' home. You would see that shit on channel six that night! John Knicely would be like, "Tyrone Washington was found guilty on all charges and thrown into the sun."

Now, those stories are ones that Lacey has witnessed. It gets even crazier when there are no Black people around. Like in these stories!

COPS GIVING THEIR ALL TO PROTECT MY FRIEND MB

My good friend MB, who is a white lady, and I love to trade opposite stories. Stories where I'm suffering some racist nonsense and she's getting away with everything but murder. It's so shocking to me. I can't believe this is happening to my little bud. Being white is hilarious. So, as you read these next five stories, try to think about how out of place they are in this book. Try to imagine a Black man getting away with any of this. It's fun because you can't!

Here are MB's stories:

Story 1, 2018
I got pulled over going fifty-five in a thirty-five. I'd had two Christmas ales and while I didn't feel intoxicated, I was

very aware that I might not pass a Breathalyzer so I quickly crammed a handful of peanut butter pretzels in my mouth, realized I didn't have any water to wash them down with, and was practically choking when the officer arrived at my window. I had my ID ready but when I started reaching for my glove box to grab my registration the officer said, "Oh, I don't need to see anything else." I was silently bargaining with my higher power, happy to get a speeding ticket in exchange for not having to do a field sobriety test.

> **Him:** Do you know how fast you were going?
> **Me:** I do not, but I totally trust that I was speeding and I'm so sorry.
> **Him:** You were going fifty-five in a thirty-five. At first I couldn't tell if it was you or the silver car in front of you, but then you passed him.
> **Me:** Oh yes. Again, I'm so sorry!
> **Him:** Okay, I'll just give you a warning this time. Happy Holidays.

He did not write me a warning, run my license, ask if I'd been drinking, or any other incriminating questions. The whole interaction was over in less time than it had taken me to find a good spot to pull over.

Story 2, 2019

I had done an improv show in Toledo, about sixty miles away from my home. I do not like to drive at night as I'm prone to falling asleep at the wheel. After the show I felt awake enough to make it home, and brushed off my friend's offer for me to crash at their house. When my GPS did not navigate me to the turnpike but instead a series of winding back roads I was in trouble. With less than ten miles to go I was rolling my windows down, blasting eighties hair metal, and slapping myself in the face. Nothing was working. I was nodding off. I got pulled over not far from my house. I'd almost made it. It was just after 1:00 a.m. The officer said I was going forty-five in a thirty-five, and I'd drifted left of center.

> *Him:* Is everything all right? You were speeding and drifting left of center.
> *Me:* I'm so sorry. I think I started to doze off. I shouldn't be driving at night.
> *Him looking at my license:* Do you still live at this address?

I nod yes.

> *Him:* Why don't I escort you the rest of the way home? I'll follow you and make sure you get home safely.

And that is what he does. He writes me a warning for the speeding but doesn't ask if I've been drinking, or if I'm on drugs or anything else that one might suspect of a person who is driving poorly at one o'clock on a Sunday morning. He also never looks at my vehicle registration or proof of insurance.

The following week my friend Talon calls me upset he's just gotten a speeding ticket on his lunch break from working as the community outreach coordinator at city hall. He was apparently going thirty in a twenty-five. I ask if he's got the ticket handy and he does. We compare notes and it's the EXACT SAME OFFICER who drove me home instead of citing me for far more serious infractions. Now, I'm sure you'll be shocked to learn that Talon is a young Black man and I am still a middle-aged white lady. I'm literally curious how far I could push it before I got in trouble? Like can I just politely take things from stores? Can I announce that I'm not going to pay my bill at a restaurant and then just leave? I suspect the answer is—probably? IDK.

Story 3, 2014

I'm driving from LA to East Texas to attend a wedding. I'd stopped for the night in El Paso and had about eleven hours to go so I got a pretty early start. A little less than an hour into the drive and I find myself at what appears to be a border crossing. *Oh no*, I think, *I've gone the wrong way and now I'm headed to Mexico!* I'm kicking myself for the lost time, but I'm also nervous. I'm driving the vehicle I currently live in, a 2010 Honda CRV. This vehicle is suspicious for at least a dozen reasons. One, everything I own is inside, with a small space carved out for me to sleep in the back. Two, it has dealer plates from Illinois, an expired registration, and I am carrying an Ohio driver's license. Three, on my travels I have visited Colorado and Oregon and have some substances that, while legal in those states, I am not supposed to transport across state lines. The thrust of traffic forces me closer to the border agents and there is nowhere to turn around. As I get closer I get more panicked.

The border agent waves me through, but I roll down my window anyway.

> **Me:** Am I lost? I'm not trying to go to Mexico today. I'm trying to drive east.
> **Him:** Nope, you're all right. Go on through.
> **Me:** No, I don't think you understand. I do not want to go to Mexico.
> **Him, becoming more exasperated:** Please pull through. You're all good.
> **Me:** Is this a border crossing?
> **Him:** No, it's a checkpoint. You are clear to proceed.
> **Me:** A checkpoint? What's that mean?
> **Him:** We are checking for illegal activity. Your vehicle is fine. Please pull through.
> **Me:** So I'm not going to Mexico?
> **Him, very upset:** Ma'am, you are in Texas, about a hundred miles from the border and we have no reason to suspect illegal activity in your vehicle. Please pull through. You are backing up the line.

I did some research and found out that border patrol in the US has the right to set up checkpoints anywhere within a hundred-mile-perimeter of our border. This law allowed agents to arrest and deport sixty farm workers in my hometown of Sandusky, Ohio, in 2018. The farm workers were all from South America, but because Sandusky sits on Lake Erie it is less than one hundred miles from the Canadian border and therefore subject to patrol. I also learned that in the Southwest US checkpoints regularly detain and harass Latinx looking drivers who have all the proper documentation, disrupting the lives of people who have to traverse these highways daily to get to and from work or school. They have to allow extra time in their commute to be harassed. It's exhausting. Meanwhile, I was absolutely breaking several laws, and my presence was seen as a nuisance instead of a threat.

Story 4, 2020

I'm bartending at a brewery on Catawba Island. Two women in their late sixties arrive very intoxicated. When the drunker of the two tries to order, my coworker politely tells her that it's close to closing time and he's happy to call them a cab, but he can't serve them. She becomes irate. She starts asking for the manager and quickly moves on to throwing her tantrum at the security cameras. She is cussing and yelling and flipping off the staff and cameras. She's spouting nonsense and wacky QAnon conspiracy theories. Our manager tells her that she needs to leave immediately. I run out the back door to the parking lot and call 911. I report the woman's behavior and tell the dispatcher I'm going to read her the license plate of the woman's vehicle because I believe she is too drunk to drive.

At this point three men (two white guys and a black guy, all late forties, early fifties) who've been sitting at the bar most of the evening come out to the parking lot and walk toward their motorcycles. The drunk woman begs for a ride. The men decline. She gets on the back of one of their bikes anyway. The man seems annoyed (I'm not sure) but gives her a ride around the parking lot. This is when the cops show up. And you'll NEVER believe who they immediately approach. JK, you totally believe it. It's the Black man on his motorcycle. I and the other employees tell the officers that it's the two older white ladies who were being drunk and disruptive. The cops completely calm down. They talk to the women for less than two minutes before letting them get in their car and drive away. I pick my jaw up off the parking lot pavement and head back inside to finish work.

We all joke about the QAnon lady being some senator's wife or something. But honestly, she's probably just a regular old white lady.

Story 5, 2020

My cousin Paul and I are returning from a very wild overnight in Tijuana. He is driving my car back to Los Angeles while I am hungover in the passenger seat. Paul is Latino and gay. He is driving close to ninety in a sixty-five when we pass a cop on a motorcycle. The cop is not parked like a speed trap. He is just driving, and we pass him. We get pulled over. The cop is really giving Paul a hard time.

> *Cop:* You make me look like an asshole
> when you drive by me that fast and don't
> slow down. You give me no choice. I

don't want to pull you over, but I don't want to look like a fucking asshole.

Paul: I'm sorry, Officer.

Cop: It's disrespectful. You're making me look bad. I have to pull you over.

Me: Officer, I'm so sorry. This is actually all my fault. This is my car and my cousin was so kind to offer to drive me home because I have a migraine. He's so worried about me that I don't think he realized how fast he was going. I'm sure he was just trying to get me home safely and if he'd seen you, he would have slowed down. We didn't mean any dis-respect.

Cop: Okay, I'm gonna give you a warning this time, but seriously, if you see us out here on the highway, you gotta slow down.

And that brings us to the end of MB's stories. MB is wild and if you get a chance to hang with her, you should. Especially if you want to see white privilege in action! I gotta send this girl that trophy.

CHAPTER EIGHT

LOOK AT THESE DICKS

Here's a fun mix of stories that we hate equally. Except for the last one in this chapter. That one is sad. So just know that as you read this you will have a fun and then sad time.

FUNNEST LOOK-ALIKE

I was in the department store Von Maur picking out a few things before my next visit to New York. I'm walking around the store and the lady that's helping me asks what I'm shopping for. I tell her I'm on my way to New York and I'm looking for some fun pieces. She's curious and asks why I'm going to New York, and I end up telling her about my book. A coworker of hers sees me and comes right over and asks if I'm the lady who wrote the book about racism. We all end up having a great conversation and they end with how they just can't believe that this stuff happens to me all the time. I tell them I wish it didn't but it's all true.

I leave their area and go to another part of the store. The store will be closing soon, so I'm frantically searching for black pants. I can't find the ones I love. A woman behind the counter says, "Is everything okay?" I tell her, "No I'm searching for a certain pair of black pants. I'm going to New York tomorrow for work, so I really need them." The woman says "New York? But you work here!" I tell her, "I don't work here." And she says "Yes, you do." To be clear, this woman, a perfect stranger, is telling me, a lady she doesn't know, where she works. Guys, I try to convince her she's wrong but it cannot be done. She was so sure of herself that I honestly was like, *Dang. Maybe I do work here.*

As soon as it goes from a more fun, "I think you're mistaken" type of "I don't work here" to a more insistent, "I DO NOT WORK HERE" it happens. Directly in between the two of us, walks a Black lady pushing a cartful of clothes. The employee was, and I think this is the only correct use of this word—gobsmacked. Her head keeps swiveling back and forth at us like she's watching a tennis match. She can't believe her eyes are deceiving her like this. I knew immediately this was my department store twin. I laugh so hard directly in this woman's face and run over to the Black lady. I introduced myself and tell her, "I know the store is closing soon but I just have to tell you what just happened." She laughs and laughs as I tell her how her timing couldn't have been more perfect when she walked between us and how her coworker insisted I worked here. We both agree it's the hair and then laugh some more because we realized this lady can't believe more than one Black person could be wearing an Afro in Von Maur. I asked her if I could take a pic of us for the next book and she said yes! I take our picture, buy my pants, and make my way back to the first ladies who were so fun to talk to. I tell them the story, we have a good laugh, and they realize this stuff really does happen to me all the time. I'm a magnet! A horrible, no-fun magnet!

WORST COPS

So, I had just moved and I'm loving my new home and the neighborhood. On my third night there I'm up late watching a movie and my daughter has already fallen asleep next to me on the couch. It's about 1:30 a.m., and I hear a car honking. I don't give it a second thought because I know it can't be for me. This honking continues for about fifteen minutes so I finally get up and take a look outside. There is a big, brand-new SUV parked right in front of the house on the street. I have no idea who this person is so I still think, *This can't be for me.* I go back to my movie and the honking goes on for another fifteen minutes. Then it finally stops. I go to look out my window and a man is walking up to my door. He starts to knock on my door and then very quickly he starts beating on it loudly and trying to pull it open. I call the police. The operator on the phone asks what my emergency is, I tell her there is a man beating loudly on my door and trying to get in. She's taking me seriously and I'm delighted. She asks if I have a description. I tell her I can clearly see he is a white male with long blond hair wearing a black hoodie. I swear to you her voice eases up and she asks, "Well, do you know him?" Really? You think I wouldn't have led with *Hello, Ken Winklebaum is trying to beat down my door. Here is his personal information.* "Do you know him," as if this makes the situation less dangerous? Would you like to see the numbers on that? I guarantee you will not like them.

I tell the operator that I do not know him and I ask if she can please send someone right away. I give her my address. She says there is a car in the area and someone should be there shortly. And then while a strange man is literally beating down my door, she HANGS UP. I call her back. I tell the operator I'm not sure about the Omaha Police call center, but in the movies they stay on the line with you. Now this stranger has walked around my house, opened up my gate, and is trying to get into my back door. I tell her what's happening and ask, "When is the car coming?" She said, "They will be here soon." This man is banging and yelling at my back door for what seems like forever when he suddenly stops. I'm wondering if he has given up, but then all of a sudden he is trying to get in my front door again. Now, remember when I told you my daughter was sleeping on the couch? She is the soundest sleeper in the world. I have planted myself in front of my door with my knife.

Oh, if you know me, you know, I have a knife. Her name is Stabitha.

So Stabitha and I are chilling there, seeing if this guy is going to make it through. After what could've been four thousand murders, my daughter gets up and says, "What's going on?" I tell her there is a white guy trying to beat down the door but I don't think he can get through, plus the police are on their way. She falls right back to sleep. Guys, if America ever enters the sleep Olympics, my child will bring home the gold.

So, this man suddenly stops again and now I watch him walk to the nice old lady's house across the street. He starts beating on her front door. I tell the operator that now he is at a neighbor's house doing the same thing. I watch him go back and forth to the front and back door over and over. The police still have not shown up. He then comes out to the sidewalk and lays spread eagle out on the grass. Maybe he got tired from all that attempted breaking and entering? I have no answers for you there. I'm just telling you how this all went down. So, I'm giving the operator the play-by-play and still asking where the police are. I thought they were in the area. All of a sudden he jumps up, hops in his car, and drives away. At that exact moment the police drive down the street and pass him. They realize this is the guy and turn around and follow him. It has been twenty-two minutes. It took them twenty-two minutes to get to me. Thank goodness this man wasn't the smartest intruder. Because a better one could have definitely made it into my home with that kind of time. They have been gone for four minutes when I see them coming back to my home. I'm assuming I will see this man in the back of the police car. I don't. The two officers walk up to my door, a white man and woman. They tell me they did catch up with the guy. I'm thrilled. "Where is he?" They tell me, "Oh he was from Iowa, he was lost."

So, I'm absolutely livid. I talk to them in a way I have never talked to a cop in my entire life. And, I probably won't again but if you put my child in danger, this is the least you can expect. I say, "What? You let him go? Which one of those things gave him permission to try to break into my house? The fact that he was lost or the fact that he was from Iowa? What are the rules? You need to tell me because I'm confused." They are silent. They can see the anger and amazement on my face when I ask, "So did you check his ID? Did you make him get out of the car? Was he under the influence? Because his behavior indicated to me that he was under the influence of likely a few things. Did you get the description of what he was doing from dispatch? Do you even know he tried to break into my home? Was he carrying a weapon? Because what if he returns when you guys leave and he has a weapon? I gotta wait another twenty-two minutes for you to come back here and give him a prize? Please tell me you searched him. I'm sitting here with my daughter and this man tries to break into my home and you tell me he is lost from Iowa? This is the best you can do?" I am both furious and sure these cops are gonna lose it on me. But, they don't. I look at the officers and I can tell both of them are a little embarrassed. They just try to reassure me that they think he is harmless. Harmless. That word pushed the last bit of common sense out of my mind, and I say to these people what we are all thinking. I tell them, "You know if that had been a Black man in a hoodie, there are a hundred other outcomes that could have happened. The best of them being him in the back of your patrol car for trespassing and an attempted break in. There is no way you would have let a Black man go for this. You would have immediately asked him to step out of his car and you would have done a search. So, I see right now how it works when I call the police in this neighborhood which is predominantly Black. Twenty-two minutes? I could have been dead. As a single mother I don't feel safe. I think I'm going to need to purchase a security system and a very large dog because calling the police here is pretty disappointing." The woman just looks at me and I know she can tell I'm right. The man just says, "I'm sorry you feel that way." Two days later I ended up getting my security system and my 130-pound Great Dane, Izzy. That was almost four years ago and I'm glad to say nothing like that has ever happened again.

I guess the moral of the story is, if it's two in the morning and you're from Iowa and you have long, blond hair, find a house and try to break into it! It's your right!

MOST RACIST SECURITY GUARDS

When I attended Central High School, we would often go to the mall downtown and hang out after school. It was one of my favorite places to meet my friends. Inside was the most delicious cookie shop, and I would often stop by. They knew me well in that store because I'm a dang cookie fiend. The staff was giggly and fun. Always very pleasant. One day when I stopped by the cookie shop the lady behind the counter says, "They are not going to allow students into the mall anymore after school, I'm so sorry, I just wanted to give you a heads-up. It makes no sense to me because you guys always buy my cookies, and I haven't had any problems, but I don't make the rules here." I'm devastated and I ask when this rule is going into effect. She says she doesn't know. I'm so sad but I make sure to tell my friends we'd better enjoy it here as much as we can because we won't be able to for much longer. We have a few last cookie parties, and later on that week the signs go up on the doors: "No Students Allowed." I'm crushed.

Then, I see students still going in. And I think, *Maybe they're not enforcing it yet!* These white students walked right in without a problem. I'm by myself getting ready to just go home but I think, *Maybe just one cookie.* I go in. Now, something you need to know about me is that I didn't look like your average student.

I'll take this description. Lacey was always dressed like Dominique Deveraux from *Dynasty*. Fucking shoulder pads, pantyhose, and pumps. The height of late eighties fashion. Pantyhose and pumps to school. Guys. I can't.

You're just jealous.

Pantyhose and pumps, that was my favorite thing to wear. Make fun of my clothes if you want, Amber, I'm still hoping they bring pantyhose back.

Don't hold your breath.

So, since I looked nothing like a student, the security guards walked right past me. They also walked right past the white students. They make a beeline for the Black students who also came in. They start harassing the young Black male students and they are aggressive as hell. Cursing, pushing, and grabbing at them, I honestly never saw anything like this in my life. I'm frozen in fear wondering how far this is going to go. Some of the kids walk out immediately but some are demanding that security not put their hands on them. This only makes security even more angry. Grown men pick up these boys and literally throw them out the door. I mean, they physically lift several boys off their feet and throw them out onto the sidewalk. I remember looking a young boy in the eye as he was being pulled by his jacket and as he struggled to get away, he fell down the stairs.

At this point I'm afraid they may find out I'm a student and I'll be next. I go back to the cookie store and ask the lady if I can stay inside till it's safe to leave. She tells me I can stay as long as I like and not to worry. During all of this, I never saw them go after one white student. So, I think we know why the signs were really put up. When I see that it's safe, I thank the store clerk and I walk calmly to the nearest exit. Black people being thrown out of a building while white people stand and watch. Reminds you of a certain time in history, right? Except this was in the nineties. As I leave, I know I will never go back inside that place again.

WORST DJ

I'm at work and we are all waiting for our meeting to start and one of my coworkers—let's call him Kirby—decides to play some music while we wait for everyone to arrive. There are a hundred reasons why this is a bad idea. Hello, anyone out there listening who has a meeting that they have to attend at work: please don't do this. Not everyone is going to agree on your choices and it's just an all-around bad idea. This fool looks me dead in the eye and says, "Lacey, I know you're going to like this." I freeze inside because I know exactly what he is going to play. Some rap with the n-word laced throughout the song and then I'll have to tell him that's not really appropriate for work and can he turn it off. Or, it'll be rap with the n-word in it and he'll rap along and I'll go to jail for slapping him.

To my surprise it's rock and I'm like, *Okay, I wasn't expecting that.* I listen to all kinds of music, so I don't say anything at first and then I'm like, *Wait . . . stop. Is this? Yes, it is.* He is playing me "Brown Sugar" by the Rolling Stones. Now if you don't know what this song is, let me ruin it. It's about Africans that were sold to a plantation in New Orleans and raped by the white enslaver. Listen, I'm not here to debate with anyone about whether or not this song sounds good. Should it still be played or should it even have been written? Don't care. Got bigger fish to fry. I'm just saying don't turn to the only Black person in the room and dedicate this song to them in front of everyone.

DJ VOICE
Hey everybody, you're listening to the rockin' sounds of DJ Kirby Kirb and this song goes out to Lacey Lamar while she is sitting in the morning meeting minding her own damn business!
AIR HORN

I tell Kirby, "I do know this song, and I really don't want to hear it. You may think it's great, but it truly does not need to be played at work in a meeting. Listen to this song in your office with your headphones on and the door shut. I'm not here to debate. Can we start the meeting now?" Kirby turns the song off. It was a short but bad DJ career.

WORST AT GIVING RAISES

So I'm working at a very nice retirement home, and I befriended Tiffany, one of the only Black housekeepers. She is so much fun and we have the best conversations. I make it a point to find her whenever I come in and ask her how her day is going and see if she needs anything. One day at work I overheard her direct supervisor talking about how they lucked out hiring her. I chime in and say, "Right, she is so nice and does a great job." "Oh, that's not what we are talking about." They look at each other and start to snicker. I say, "Okay, what are you talking about, then?" They say, "We are saving so much money having her work here. She only makes nine dollars an hour." My daughter made more than that at her first job at a coffee shop. I'm trying not to show my disgust as I ask, "Wow, how long has she worked here?" I cannot believe it when I find out this woman has worked faithfully for this company for fourteen years. They are just giggling with pride at how they have kept this Black woman at an unlivable wage for fourteen years and thought I would be laughing right along with them. I tell them how horrible that is, how disgusting they are, and how I can't believe she is still working there. Fourteen years and she is only making nine dollars an hour? I go straight to find her and ask her if this is true and she says yes. I ask her if she wants me to see if I can get her more pay and she says yes. I tell her, as a director, I can try. I tell her she could be making a lot more money at virtually any other place and if she doesn't get a raise she really should look into leaving because this just isn't right. So, I end up meeting with HR and her supervisor about getting her more pay. They are absolutely against it and can't imagine why I would be trying to make the company pay more money to this employee. I'm livid but Tiffany does not want to ruffle any more feathers and thanks me for trying. With the help of Amber, I end up getting Tiffany a part-time job outside of work that pays her MORE than her main job. Let me repeat that, she ends up with a part-time job that pays more than her current job. I slap each of my coworkers right in the face. Okay, I didn't but the thought of doing that sustained me for the rest of my time there!

WORST RACIST COMMENT I WAS NOT A PART OF

One time I worked at a bank where my immediate supervisor was a very nice Vietnamese lady. She was literally one of the last people who made it to the helicopter from Vietnam at the end of the war. She was evacuated but her parents died. It always struck me that she had one of the saddest stories I'd ever heard and somehow ended up here alongside people who couldn't begin to imagine such hardship, myself included. So, our boss would make Asian jokes all the time about her eyes and rice. And we would say to her, why do you let him say this stuff? She would say, "He's just being funny," and brush it off.

Sidenote: This is a practice that never ends well. I know it may be uncomfortable to ask people to stop making racist jokes but you have to. For

your own sanity. It never goes, racist jokes—
fewer racist jokes—no racist jokes. It only goes
racist jokes—more racist jokes—an ass
whoopin'. No one loves making racist jokes
more than white people, because they're wholly
unaware of the potential pain. They also can't
see how racist jokes are a gateway drug to
full-fledged racism.

The shitty guy was trying to explain something American to her. Something like a fishing license or something like that. Now, mind you, he was not doing a good job of explaining it and as a result, she wasn't getting it. Instead of doing a better job or letting someone else try to explain it, he turned to everyone and said, "The Asian mind can't grasp every concept. There's just some stuff she's not gonna get." You may be thinking, *How did we get from "eyes and rice" to "the Asian mind"?!* Well, that was the racism that was in his heart this whole time. With every comment he made he grew braver and braver until he was out-and-out making full racist comments. But once he said that, she finally talked to him. Unfortunately, it was too late. He went on to un-successfully run for office in Bellevue, Nebraska, 'cause he's a bitch. It just makes me so mad that this woman escaped a literal war and has to put up with this piece of shit.

Okay guys, as promised, here's the sad story. Look. We've had our fair share of fun and for one story, that's over.

MOST HEARTBREAKING CHILDREN

So, I was asked to speak about our first book at a social justice Zoom event for several boys' and girls' homes across the US. I log on a little early and there is a man who is supposed to be giving the kids tips on how to get and keep jobs. It's a pretty essential part of these children's futures. A lot of them don't have parents or people who they look up to who can impart this information. But this guy is kind of trying to maybe pull a scared straight? He's talking about how hard it is out there for people looking for jobs. He's talking about how if they step out of line the teeniest bit in the workplace, employers will not hesitate to fire them. It's like when in a movie, the cadets line up at basic training and they get a big speech about how they better do right or else. Except these aren't cadets, they're children who live in a home, for fuck's sake.

So I'm watching this man scare these children and I can see in their faces that a lot of these lies are hitting home. You are talking to a group of teenagers who are probably unsure of themselves, coming from all different backgrounds and situations, some heartbreaking, and you are already talking about firing them. These kids have heard about how they're not gonna make it their whole lives. What idiot thought it would be a good idea to scare them before they leave the only semblance of stability they've ever had? Probably some Republican.

It's my turn now and I could tell I was going to be a breath of fresh air. I start off by telling them what my book is about and then I tell a few of the funniest stories. I can't see the youth but the adults are laughing, gasping, and sometimes shaking their heads in disbelief. I spend about forty-five minutes just sharing the stories from the book and then I open it up for questions and discussion. I can now see the kids as they ask questions. The first room pops up and it is full of Black students. One boy in the front has his head in his hands and his friend next to him says, "How do you deal with it? This is so hard." The way he says, "this is so hard" breaks my heart because I really don't want to think that he could be going through anything like the stories that have happened to me in the book, but I know that's exactly the case. The other boy with his head in his hands looks up and says something to me that took my breath away. "I try not to get into arguments every day because I know where that can lead. I really don't want to fight people but dealing with racism every day makes it hard. I can only take so much." WHAT? I know that racism still exists, I know people struggle with it every day, but I did not expect this reaction. These kids enjoyed the funny stories and then the good times stopped pretty quick. They aren't laughing; they all hit me with hard questions. I realized I may be the only adult some of them knew who had been through what they're going through. I felt a panic. I had to get everything I've ever learned about racism out and into these young ears in my remaining minutes. If I had known this, I would not have told my hilarious Harriet Tubman story!

I simply was not ready for the conversation to go there so quickly and stay there. The kids started sharing about people they had to deal with every day. People who were making their lives hell at times, in and out of the group home. I worked in a similar group home—remember the "I won diversity training" idiot? Yep, he worked at a group home. Imagine having him be your adult assigned to you, tasked with taking care of a young minority. Over and over the same question is asked: "What should I do when someone is racist to me? It happens all the time!" I tell them there are several things they can do. "If it's another youth in the home I would first try to remove myself from the situation. Walk away if you can; people know that if they push certain buttons they will get a reaction from you. Walk away and tell an adult that you trust and that can help you. If it's an adult who is being racist, let them know directly that their behavior and comments are not appropriate and tell someone. Talk to supervisors and other adults who work there until someone listens. You should not be living in a racist environment. You deserve to live in a place that knows how to take care of you and I'm sorry that's not the case for everyone here."

I take it a step further and say, "I know you just had a talk about employment as well, and yes it's important for you to be professional at work but it's not your job to put up with racism. Your employers had better be professional, too. Speak up if you are being treated unfairly and don't be afraid to stick up for yourselves and others." They asked me if it was scary speaking up at school and work, and I told them that sometimes it was but as I became older and more confident it became easy for me to stand up for myself. I knew my self-worth. A lot of them told me they would try to stay strong and to make the right decisions and they looked forward to reading the book. I felt like I had moved the needle on their hope. It felt good.

Right before my talk was over, a young white teenager said she had a message she wanted to share with everyone. This child started to give the longest, wrongest speech of all time. This new human being says to solve most of these problems you just shouldn't say anything. Just don't respond to people and turn the other cheek. It just makes everything easier. She knows it's the right thing to do 'cause that's what she does. When someone says something bad to her she ignores it and it goes away. Lord Jesus help us. I look at the audience and there is a young Black girl watching who looks like she is going to explode, her face is one of disbelief. I can tell what she is thinking. It's the same thing I'm thinking. Meanwhile, white teenager is not done. "You are creating more of a problem and you will get yourself into trouble by reacting to racism. If you just ignore it and don't say anything, this will end racism." Who would have guessed that the solution to racism would be bestowed upon us by a white teenager? Or that the solution was to shut up and take it?! Several of the youth start to get agitated and the moderator tells me my time is up but he is wrong. It is very not. I say as nicely as I can muster, "Oh no, excuse me. I have to address that speech. Silence is not the key to ending racism. Yes, some-times to keep yourself safe, walking away could be the best response but remaining silent at all times about racism will not end it. Be safe and do what you can to help yourself and others." Also, a little less nicely, I send a message to the group home staff. "Your group home should be your safe space. I would hope that staff is also doing everything they can to stop racism when they see it." Then, I flip right back to nice for, "That's why I'm glad you are having this social justice event today!" I can see the faces of some of the youth relax and they are so happy I added that. I'm still saddened about the boy with his head in his hands and wonder what these kids are going through every day. I'm hoping staff listened to this, too, and took steps to make their living situations better. These real kids have to live like this and I still think about it. Dang. I think we need a palate cleanser.

It may be time for us to share a long-standing Ruffin tradition with you. Putting babies in wigs and taking pictures of them. Behold:

At the Ruffin house there's always a cute little baby, and there's always a wig.

And, when you're lucky, the two of them meet.

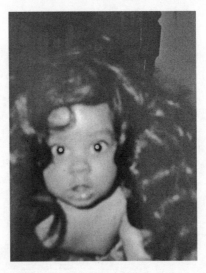

Each baby pulls off each wig effortlessly.

You have to do a double take and say, "Whoa. Was that baby born with the fullest head of hair or is that a wig?"

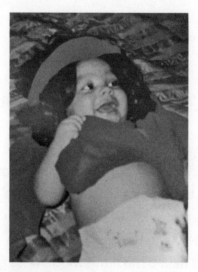

Don't worry folks. It's a wig.

CHAPTER NINE

COMMISERATING FEELS FINE!

I know what you're thinking. *Lacey, it must be so sad for you to be the only person with stories like these.* Well, I'm not! And to prove it, here are some stories from some good friends of ours!

These two are from my little friend Jill.

SECOND WORST BAR PATRON

I was eating lunch with a friend over winter break at a downtown bar and grill. I had on a sweatshirt that read "Black Is a Blessing" on the front and "God Is Dope" on the back. I had to use the restroom a couple of times, so I passed a gentleman at the bar whenever I went. One of the times, he stopped me and asked me if the wings were good. They were basic, so I told him they were okay. I didn't think anything of it, and after a while he left.

My friend and I were still there a couple of hours later

because we hadn't seen each other in a while and had a lot to catch up on. As we are chatting, the same man walked in again with his wife. He commented about us holding down the fort and offered to buy us a drink. He sat down at a table extremely close to ours. My friend and I were finishing up our chat so we welcomed them.

While having a random conversation, the man looked at me and said, "Now why would you wear that shirt?" My friend tried to change the subject, but I circled back because he asked the question and I really wanted to give him an answer. I'm not going to bore you with it 'cause if you're this deep into this book, you know why I wore the shirt. After my response he replied, "Wow, you are really smart!" This man had the gall to be shocked about it. He was shocked that I was smart and I was done with this conversation. I then mentioned to the waitress that I would buy my own drinks. But he insisted I take him up on his offer. He then went on to ask me how I would feel if a white person wore a shirt like that. I tell him, "Society tells you you're beautiful all the time. You were raised thinking white is the standard of beauty. Black people are told the opposite. So, I have no problem reminding everyone that we are beautiful."

After staying another hour, I had to move my car because the meter would not accept any more money from me. When I came back in, he looked at me in disgust and asked why I had returned. Mind you, he came in and sat at my table without an invitation.

WORST BAR PATRONS

One day I was at a local bar watching the Nebraska football team play. I was the only Black person in there, but being from Nebraska, I am not new to being the only Black person in an establishment. This particular bar I went to enough to know the regulars.

I was not there very long before the backup quarterback threw a touchdown pass. After multiple losing seasons, and being at the end of another one, beating our neighboring state rival would have given us a small reason to hold our heads up high. When they scored, all the fans had a little more hope.

The place went wild, and we all cheered! Everyone was screaming in a celebratory way when the yelling took a terrible turn. It started to morph into "Let's go Brandon! Fuck Joe Biden!" Now, it wasn't 100 percent racist, just 100 percent Republican, which I can handle. I just looked around like, "Wow." And this chanting goes on for a while. I can feel it become more pointed. Now I noticed two gentlemen at the bar looking uncomfortable and displeased with the situation. But a lot of people are on board. One person yelled, "Oh yeah, Black lives matter!" and after his friends looked at him confused, his response was, "Well there *is* a Black person in here!" Aaaand, that's when it became a race thing and I was immediately uncomfortable. Everyone realized I was there and chanted and laughed and it was not a good vibe. It was as if the place had spit me out. I packed up my stuff and went to pay for my full beer. One of the gentlemen at the bar who looked as stunned with the chanting and outbursts as I was, said it was on him. I thanked him and got the fuck out.

The next stories are from our friend, former Nebraska state senator Tanya Cook! If you look at it one way: What a cool thing for us to be able to have her in our book! But if you look at it another way: Oh no. Senators should not be in this book. BUT YOU KNOW EACH MINORITY SENATOR COULD.

Either way, thanks, Senator Cook! Each of her stories are the winners of:

MOST REGULAR DEGULAR, DAY-TO-DAY RACISM

Advocacy groups with varying levels of sophistication and organization come to the Capitol building during the legislative session. One morning, I was talking to my administrative assistant at her desk in the reception area of my office, when two bouncy, middle-aged women entered with a backpack full of goodies and flyers. "This is for the senator. Could you make sure he gets it?" They hand it to my aide, who takes it but gestures toward me, and I said, "I am she." Pregnant pause. The previously bouncy, smiley lady with the backpack full of goodies and flyers for Senator Cook reeled back on her heels. Her eyes widened. The other lady stuttered, "Are you from Omaha?" I said, "Yes, I am." Silently, they looked at me, seemingly double-checking that I'm both a woman and Black. Then, without saying another word, they turned around and left.

I was excited to be participating in the "Dance for a Chance" fundraiser for Youth Emergency Services a few years ago. This involved several weeks of rehearsing choreography and shaking down my friends and colleagues for pledges. My college girlfriends were flying in to support me, and I wanted to do my best to look the part. Each of the "contestants" received an email message suggesting a boutique that might be a good resource for dresses. Envisioning a swingy, sparkly something to complete my look, I went to the Southwest Omaha locale. No ballroom dance-y items to be found, but I did pick up a little khaki-colored coatdress. As I was paying for the dress, the clerk said, "So this must be a new and different experience for you, huh?" I looked at her with a confused expression. Did she mean the dance event? Then she said, "You know, coming here from North Omaha." Like people from North Omaha, a predominantly Black community, never leave it. It's Omaha. Everyone is everywhere. With the one exception of me ever being at that boutique again.

My third story is this: One dark and stormy summer morning, I got dressed in one of my favorite floral frocks. I wanted to do my part to brighten the day, maybe. I'd agreed to help chaperone kids from the Mandela School to a golf tournament and exhibition. I drove myself to the club and the kids got settled into the clubhouse to meet the pros and ask questions. I was sipping a cup of coffee and standing at the perimeter of the presentation when a white woman whom I'd never met or seen or engaged with in any way said to me, "That's not the right thing to be wearing here." She had a really serious look on her face like I was her employee and this advice was going to save my career.

Some days people's bs is easier to take. I just nodded

my head and kept sipping my coffee. I had a great day that day.

My fourth story is: I was minding my own business at my chair on the floor of the legislative chamber. My young white colleague walked toward me and looked at me with what appeared to be sincere concern and said, "Does your hair grow?" I replied, "Yes, I am a human being and my hair does grow. I style it short on purpose." Then, he got an attitude with me. I guess because he felt foolish. He must get an attitude a lot.

Thank you, Tanya. And here's my friend Michelle's winner for:

WORST INTERVIEW

I had graduated with my master's degree in public administration with an emphasis in nonprofit organization management. I'd also been training with Marijean Hall, national fundraising guru in fundraising strategy, opportunity analysis, development, and board engagement. So, when I applied for an upper-level position with the University of Nebraska Foundation, and made it to the third round of interviews, I thought I had it in the bag.

I walked into a conference room with dark, heavy, wooden furniture and blue walls. There was a single window to my right and it was the only light in the room. I sat near the center as there was a single chair on that side and about nine other chairs opposite.

In my navy-blue suit, hair pulled back into a tight bun—I

was confident. Nine white men entered the room. I watched as they struggled to pull the heavy chairs from the table over the plush, beige carpet. Not one of them appeared to be under seventy years old. Not one of them greeted me with a handshake or a smile.

It was awkward. I smiled and attempted to introduce myself, feeling my confidence fizzle out into the thick air around me. Not one of them introduced themselves to me. I sat patiently waiting on the first question. It was a softball one regarding the university. I'd received two degrees from University of Nebraska Omaha and was truly grateful and proud of my experience and the education I'd received.

The next question came from the oldest-looking man at the table. He had more wrinkles than skin. His hair was so thin, I could make out at least twenty age spots from my position. He cleared his throat and sat back a bit in his chair. All the others had their gaze fixed on him. He was sitting at the head of the table. I knew he must have been in charge (or thereabouts). He rested his head in one hand balanced on the arm of the chair, one bony finger crept up his cheek.

Then he spoke. "I'm just going to ask the question that needs to be asked here and not waste any more of anyone's time. Miss..." He finally looked at me. "...do you honestly believe that donors, old curmudgeons like me, would actually put a check in *your* hand?"

There was dead silence. I knew EXACTLY what he meant. We all did. Cool as a cucumber, I responded, "I would like to think they would." But the confidence I'd walked in with was gone. There was no certainty in my voice. My palms were sweating. I clasped them together so no one would notice they might also be shaking.

Another man, directly across from me, scooted his chair back. "I think we're done here." The others followed suit and backed away from the table. I was silent as they made their way to the door. I stood up, straight-backed and numb. "It was nice meeting you," I said, trying to smile.

I hadn't met any of them—not one of them. I gathered my purse and keys and waited until they'd all gone, until I couldn't see a single age spot. I wobbled out to the receptionist, who didn't look up at me. She said rather robotically, "You'll be notified of the decision next week."

I exited the interview knowing in my heart that the old white man was right.

CHAPTER TEN

MY SISTER THE REVEREND

Here's a few stories about my sister, Angie. Now a reverend in Minneapolis, she has a lot of experience with these types of stories. Angie has almost always been the only Black person in her workplace. The second oldest of the Ruffin children, she grew up to be the most patient reverend in the history of the world. The things these people said to her, you're not gonna believe.

WORST TACO NIGHT

One day, they have a taco night. Just a fun night where no one can get mad. Right? Nope. At this taco night, there was an old lady who was quite upset. Unfortunately, as the church vicar Angie had to ask her what was wrong. She was not prepared for her answer. The lady was mad because the cheese they put out for the tacos was Mexican. She didn't want to eat it because it was Mexican. She didn't want to eat the Mexican dish, tacos, with Mexican cheese. Which, by the way, is cheese made by Americans with some paprika in it with the word "Mexican" on the label. Her problem was not with tacos, which are Mexican, but with the word "Mexican" on the label of the cheese she was holding. This genius went on to complain, "I have basic cable and I have fifty channels. Three are in Spanish." How did we get to your cable bill from a bag of cheese? I do not know. Also, can you imagine what word would have to be on the outside of a bag of cheese for me to not eat it? Like, in order for a bag of cheese to get me to not eat it, it would have to say, "Not fit for human consumption." Even then, I'd still take a bite.

Anyway, Angie listened to this woman complain until she was finished. Then this lady scooped up the cheese and put it on her taco and went about her night. Her taco night.

SCARIEST NEIGHBOR

Growing up, the house next door had a racist white guy who lived there. When Angie was around five or six, she overheard Mom and Dad talking about how racist he was. She always made sure to steer clear of him because as a kid, you're not quite sure what "racist" means. If you used what you learned in school, being "racist" means you murdered MLK or loved owning enslaved people.

Wait. That's not what they taught in school! I learned in school that enslavers were nice to their enslaved people and they gave them food and a place to live!

You're right! Being enslaved does sound fun!

Yay!

Either way, kids didn't learn about what mainstream racism was until a little bit later. It's why a lot of white people act the way they do. They have a five-year-old's understanding of the word "racist." One day, as she was riding her bike past his house, she saw he was outside. She was almost home but terrified she was gonna get...assassinated? Discriminated? She was susceptible to new scary words whose definitions were unclear. Angie's only defense was to ride past him, unnoticed. She held her breath and rode closer and closer to him and when she was closest, Angie took a huge tumble from her bike directly at his feet. She fell off her bike and was screaming. Now she was screaming for two reasons. One, because she'd banged up her knee pretty bad and two, she was scared because she was on the ground in front of a racist. She knew she was a goner. The neighbor reached down and Angie said goodbye to the realm of the living. He then helped her up, dusted her off, and walked her back to the house. He was very nice. She learned a valuable lesson that day. The nicest people can be the biggest racists. Which, working in church, became a running theme throughout the rest of her life.

MOST TRAUMATIC MOVIE

Before I was born, two things happened.

One: Everyone in America, including my siblings, watched

the miniseries *Roots*. It was about enslaved people who were separated from their families, caged, beaten, and had their feet cut off. 10/10. I remember watching it when they re-aired it. And I was like, "My friend from *Reading Rainbow* is enslaved?!" So sorry if you don't get that reference. You grew up without *Roots* and *Reading Rainbow*. A combo that would go on to give you confidence in any actor stepping out of their genre.

Two: The whole family was in a very big car accident. Everyone was in the hospital. The whole family survived, but Mom, Dad, Angie, and Lacey are banged up pretty bad. Angie and Lacey were in the same hospital room. Angie is like seven years old which means Lacey is like four.

When Angie comes to, she's in a hospital bed. A place she's never been before. She is separated from her family and is scared. She's not sure what's happening, but she knows it's bad. Like any smart young child who has just seen *Roots*, she assumes she's been sold into slavery. Terrified, she turns and sees Lacey beside her. Lacey is in a metal cage. It's happened. Slavery is back and better than ever. Angie started screaming as loud as she could. She's terrified. Mom and Dad come in from their hospital rooms and tell her everything is fine. Lacey is in one of those old-timey metal hospital cribs. The crib is raised up. So, from Angie's point of view, it looks like a cage. It's at that point she realized no one's foot had been cut off to make it harder for them to escape and she calms down. Mom and Dad assured her that they all still owned themselves. Angie owns herself to this very day.

WORST TEACHER

In the fourth grade Angie had to do one of those "L-is-for-Love" poems. Her fourth-grade teacher accused her of plagiarizing a Hallmark card.

I IMAGINE THE POEM WENT LIKE THIS:

M is for the Magic that you possess
O is for the Only person I want to impress
T is for the Thankfulness for you that's in my heart
H is for the Hope that we shall never part
E is for Eternal, which is how long my love will last
R is for 'Resa. Mess with me, and she'll beat your ass.

(I'm gonna leave that last part out when I send Mom and Dad the book for their approval. When they see it in the final copy, Lacey will have to confess that it was her idea.)

WORST CELEBRITY LOOK-ALIKE

Angie went to college in Springfield, Missouri. It was bad. These people had never ever seen a Black person in their lives. Now, all of us probably at some point have been someone's first Black friend, but it's a lot harder to be the first Black person someone has ever laid eyes on. Once, and this is true, Angie was putting on makeup in the bathroom, and a girl came up to her and asked, "Why is your little makeup brown?" Angie said, "It's because my little face is brown." Can you believe the stupidity? The girl asked why a brown person's makeup was brown. If you ask me, Angie should have run screaming from this place right then. But it would take a little longer for that to happen.

One day, at that school, there's a church event of some kind and Angie realizes she is the only Black person there. At a church event. In Missouri. She knows she's in for it. A young white couple comes up to her and says, "You remind me of a movie star." Now, it's the nineties. Ain't but like three Black woman movie stars at this point and Angie doesn't look a thing like any of them. She starts to hightail it away from them.

> ***Angie:*** Thank you. (She turns around and
> starts moving.)
> ***White Couple:*** Don't you wanna know
> who it is? (They're in pursuit.)
> ***Angie:*** No thank you. (She's moving
> faster now.)
> ***These Motherfuckers:*** What? (They
> catch up to her.)
> ***ANGIE:*** No. I don't want to know. (The
> fact that these people are unable to read
> her moving very quickly away from them
> as a clue she doesn't want to be in this
> conversation tells Angie that, socially,
> these guys are not where they need to be
> to be talking to her.)

These people corner her and prove her right.

The Two Dumbest People in Missouri:
Have you ever seen the movie _Gone with the Wind_?

Oh god. We all know what's coming. Angie is a very cute eighteen-year-old kid. Hattie McDaniel was forty-five when she was in that movie. To tell a child she looks forty-five is very super bad. It's not really the biggest compliment. Now, at this point, they can tell by her body language that she hates it.

> **_[Turner Classic Idiots]:_** No, we were gonna say Hattie McDaniel!
> **_Angie:_** (in her mind) You fucking idiots. (out loud) That's not a compliment.
> **_Butt Heads:_** She won an Oscar for that role!
> **_Angie:_** You didn't say I _acted_ like her. You said I _looked_ like her. And I don't. The next time you want to tell a Black person who they look like, don't.

Can you imagine being the Black woman reverend of an all-white church in a small town? Well you don't have to! Just read the rest of Angie's stories!

MOST RACIST CHURCH

In order for Angie to survive at these churches, she's got to do a few things. She has to stay calm; she has to know who has her back and who doesn't; and she has to not throw anyone out a window. I know that last one sounds easy, but you would be surprised.

We've put these stories in order of easiest to believe to hardest to believe and we are sorry you have to read them but you doooooo!

MOST SENSITIVE CONGREGANT

It was around 2014. Angie worked at a church in Waukesha, Wisconsin. Why? So, we could write this book, of course! So, the church is full of "call the cops on you 'cause you're sharing the same space" types. This is not how Angie would put it. She'd say something more like, "It was a challenge for them to have a Black, female reverend." Isn't that nice? Angie is nice. To a point. Anyhoo, in this church, an old white lady asked to talk to Angie. She went through the trouble of making an appointment. That's how you know it's going to be something either terrible or terrible. (There aren't a lot of great meetings when you're a reverend. People don't, like, have meetings to tell you how great things are going, but they should.) This woman called this meeting with Angie because she had a huge problem with Angie's language. More specifically, that Angie was referring to the congregation as "brothers and sisters." Angie explained that the apostle Paul uses this familial language. That did not sway her. Angie explained Jesus used this language. That did not sway her. In fact, this woman said, "I just don't like you saying that even though I know it's probably cultural." There it is. Somehow

169

when every other priest, pastor, and reverend says it, it's fine, but when Angie says it, it's cultural? The previous reverend opened the service every Sunday by singing, "I greet you as your brother and your servant." He looked her in the eyes every Sunday and called himself her brother. She had not complained about that. Yet, this bitch made an appointment to see Angie.

It's at this point, I am required to note that Angie is against me calling her former congregants names. And, I speak for me, Lacey, and everyone reading it when I say, "We understand you do not approve of these raggedy little bitches being referred to WITH THE TRUTH."

This is a beautiful demonstration of the extent to which racism goes. You can literally say the same words as a white person and be misunderstood. Angie explains it's not cultural. If God is Angie's father and your father then that makes us sisters. And this woman's reply was, "Yes, but it makes me uncomfortable." Angie explained that there was nothing she could do about that. The woman explained she just wanted her to note her being uncomfortable with it. That next Sunday, Angie said her normal "brothers and sisters in Christ." But what she wanted to say was "Brothers and sisters in Christ…and Nettie Jay." Angie never stopped saying it. Well, she didn't stop saying it back then. Now, she says "siblings of the faith" because we learned about being gender nonbinary. But back when we were idiots, Angie made sure to say "brothers and sisters."

MOST RACIST GHOST

Angie worked at a church in Delphos, Ohio. Now, this was Delphos, Ohio. Arguably the worst place Angie has ever worked. The most racist city she has ever lived in. Her stories from this place will really hurt a person's feelings. So, in Delphos (Hell-phos) one of her congregants died. He was a very old man with a very old family. His family came in and asked that someone else officiate his funeral. "Dad wouldn't have liked having a Black person preside at his funeral." Bitch, he's dead! What the fuck is he gonna do? File a complaint? Nuts that the guy got to be racist from BEYOND THE GRAVE! Spooooky discriminaaaatioooon!

Angie explained she was as white and as male as she was ever going to get, and that they were out of luck. So, the family tried the next Lutheran church. It was all the way in Fort Wayne, Indiana. Surely, their reverend would hear their sad story and save them. Well guess what?! Their reverend was ALSO A BLACK WOMAN NAMED ANGIE! And, at this point I have to say, how beautiful. The Lord works in mysterious and hilarious ways. So, they were forced to make do with Angie. But, here's the thing. Angie doesn't want to do this funeral if everyone there's gonna be mad. A funeral for a racist is bound to have racists in attendance and, in a way, this is just like sending her to the wolves. Yes, these people are gross and wrong but some old man's funeral isn't the place to have a teachable moment. So, Angie asked the local retired reverend to do it. He tells Angie they offered to "pay him handsomely" and for that reason he couldn't do it. "It wouldn't be right." Angie said, "So, you're going to send

171

me in there?" And he said, "It's not right for me to do it." So, here's the problem with that. This man "meant well" but was only concerned with himself. He doesn't know how to handle racism. Angie does. He can't see the whole picture. Angie can. What ended up happening was Angie's presiding over this funeral and it activated local racists and helped build up resentment toward Angie. Resentment that led to some real messed-up shit. So, in short, that's the problem with people who "mean well." And that was one racist ass ghost.

MOST MACRO MICROAGGRESSIONS

When Angie worked at what she thought of as a very progressive church, they had a whole workshop about micro-aggressions. Angie thought, *Wow. This must be some place to work if they're already talking about microaggressions!* Every other place she'd worked up to this point needed a workshop on why you couldn't just hop on a Black person's back and have them give you a piggyback ride to your desti-nation. So, she attended this workshop and people from the congregation *actually came*. She was floored. They talked at length about what a microaggression actually was, different types of them, and how they could hurt. At the get-together afterward, an older white woman approached Angie. This woman, fresh out of the workshop went, "I know we just had a workshop about microaggressions where they said you can't touch Black people's hair, but I just have to do this." And then exactly what you thought was gonna happen happened. This woman Angie did not fucking know got into her dreads with both hands and shook them, saying, "See, that wasn't so painful now, was it?" This bitch *just* learned it was wrong, decided to do it anyway, and insisted it was an okay thing to do. Guys. Angie is just a person. She's made of flesh and bone just like you and I. She murdered this woman right there in cold blood. At that point, all the Black people in town ripped off their clothes to reveal jazzy white loincloths and sang "Brand New Day." Just kidding. Angie, new to the job and still figuring out if this was a "get fired if you make white women cry" kind of church or "you can be a full human being" kind of church simply replied, "It wasn't my favorite." So, if you get to heaven and Angie isn't there, it can only be because she ain't dead yet.

WORST CHURCH QUOTES

These are things said to Angie at church. Guaranteed to make you wanna fight. Especially this first one:

"I love Black people. My granddaddy sells them."

"Shoot that n-word pastor." (I'M SO SORRY. IT DID HAPPEN. TECHNICALLY, IT HAS TO GO IN HERE.)

"Pastor, I wanna ask you a question, why are your kids so ugly?" Now, Angie is a pretty cool guy, but this comment made her prepared to lose her job. Angie was ready to fight. She made no effort to hide her anger as she replied, "My kids are gorgeous." The woman looked terrified as she said, "Oh I know I was just...," and Angie, child of God, walked away. And, can I just point out how perfect these children are? Each one cuter than the last. Angie may be all about heaven, but her children are

Cute

As

Hell!!

Angie's husband had made friends with two old white men from church. Frankly, it was a small town, and he didn't have much of a choice. So, he had made a date to go fishing with them. Angie walked by and they said to her, "Excited to go fishing with Benhi this weekend! Tell Benhi to bring the fish bait!" and they fell out laughing. Now, at this point, Angie should've called it an unusually great interaction with Statler and Waldorf* and kept it moving. But she had to know what it meant. She walked up to them and said, "What does that mean? 'Bring the bait'?" Waldorf leans in close and says, "You know"—he grabs her dreads and shakes them—"make sure you bring the fish bait!"

---

* Do you get that reference? If so, please tweet at Angie, "Muppets gonna Muppet." Also, in the last book, I had a few of these in here where I jokingly asked readers to tweet stuff at me and Lacey and every time people actually did it, I laughed out loud. You're fun.

GRAMMAR POLICE

A father is giving testimony at church and he is talking about how he and his daughter were singing some hymn with the word "ain't" in it. He said that as they were singing, she stopped the song to tell him they needed to sing it "correctly." The child refused to sing it as it was written. And the father was very proud of his tiny Elvis Presley of a child who can "fix" this Black song. Angie was in the very, very back of the church and stood up and left. Their correcting a spiritual was more than she could take on that day. She went home.

THAT'S NOT A MICROAGGRESSION, THIS IS A MICROAGGRESSION

At some church social type of thing, Angie is talking about the dangers of microaggressions and how they can turn into macroaggressions and how those can then turn into murder. In general, she's talking about the safety of Black people. Then, a member of her church who is really gung ho about the environment in an aggressive way told everyone it's the same as the environment. Racism is the same as the environment. Angie decided to explore this new fun theory and tried to explain how it's a privilege to focus on the environment when people are dying. This is a specific type of racism. Like, when white people equate any old discomfort they feel to racism. It truly boggles the mind. Anyway, aggro environment lady will not budge. She let them know she had a story that would clear things up. Angie knew it wouldn't but she had to hear how crazy this was gonna get. The enviromentress explained how she'd driven cross-country in an electric car, and she forgot her water bottle. And, and this is true, she talked about how she was forced to buy a plastic water bottle and reuse it for the whole trip AND WAS BROUGHT TO TEARS. She cried about having to buy a water bottle. She wanted Angie to know that she has pain too. She ended her insane ramblings with, "There are environmental micro-aggressions. See?"

Bitch, that's not what the fuck we were talking about. Also, even if that were a thing, why bring it up now? It doesn't negate what I've just said. What even is that? It's like if I was talking about cats and you were like "But dogs exist, too. See?" Yes, idiot, I know there's more than one thing in the world.

TAKES A DEEP BREATH

I wish you could see how angrily I typed that last tangent. This book really helps a person work through some shit, I swear.

MOST RACIST INCIDENTS AT SEMINARY

While she was at seminary, Angie had become addicted to cable TV because, as a promo, they got it free for three months before they had to start paying. Realizing no one was paying for it, this nerd called and confessed that they still had cable. It would be another three months before a cable guy would come to make things right. The day he was scheduled to come worked out perfectly. Everyone was supposed to be in chapel that day. Angie could sit in the back and slip out undetected, let the cable guy in, and come right back. Well, he came as everyone was talking to each other at the end. Angie rushed out, let him in, and rushed right back. And when she got back the whole place was abuzz with the drama that had unfolded. People let her know that she missed a scandal. Apparently, during chapel, some Black woman stormed out! Just grabbed all of her things and left in a big showy huff. Rumors were flying about who she was, what her problem was, and why she would do such a thing. It took a long time before she realized they were talking about her.

In 1989 at Evangel University in Springfield, Missouri, a fellow student (let's call her Jo) simultaneously asked to touch Angie's hair, while *actually* touching her hair. Jo gasps in surprise, "Oh wow, it's soft!!"

"Soft?"

Then, this fool had the nerve to say, "Yeah, I thought it would be slick. You know, like a raincoat."

Angie sat motionless in stunned silence as she pondered this. Had anyone's hair in the history of the world felt "slick like a raincoat"? Should she get a wig made out of raincoats? Could she pull it off? I mean, ha, ha, ha. That was just a joke originally, but now I'm really thinking about it.

In missionary orientation in 1999 Angie spent three weeks of torture with a group of amazingly ignorant white people, as she says, "in the name of the Lord!" She was being trained to serve as a missionary in Namibia. During the training, they had cafeteria-style meals. But at dinnertime, there was a dessert cart. One night, as it rolled by, one of the older, bitchier women says to the entire table, "Oh! The dessert cart is here! I see watermelon. Does anyone want some watermelon?" With a wave of her hand and an eye roll, she quips, "Angie, I KNOW you want some watermelon." Angie sat motionless in stunned silence wondering if she could pull off a wig made of raincoats. Just kidding. She kindly put that woman in her place "in the name of the Lord."

At seminary they would give you a list of mandatory dates. If you missed them, you don't get credit. Days you like HAD to be there. One day, a student said to Angie, "See you at the meeting tonight." Angie insisted that it wasn't tonight, but when the student said it was, Angie called the other two Black people on campus. They weren't told about it, either. It turns out, they had sent out a campus-wide email and the only people who weren't on it were the three Black students. They went and talked to the staff and watched them put them on the email chain. After they fixed the problem, it happened three more times. Someone was taking the Black people off the list. At frigging seminary.

Another time at seminary a woman complained about dirty stairs in her apartments. Angie's Namibian husband, Benhi, was working maintenance there. They send him to this woman's house to clean the stairs. This same woman who asked for the stairs to be cleaned sees a Black man cleaning the stairs that she requested to be cleaned and she calls and says, "There's a Black man in our building." This ho should've been more specific when she asked for someone to clean her stairs. Because of this, they decide that Benhi had to wear someone's old maintenance shirt. Complete with their name tag and pit stains. Angie asks Benhi what everyone else is wearing. Benhi said, "Their own clothes." And Angie went to the facilities manager and cursed him up one side and down the other. Here are some of the things she yelled (although they are funny, these are real):

"A uniform is only a uniform if everyone is wearing it. If only one person is wearing it, it's an insult."
"His mama named him Kunta and he will not be called Toby."
"If you tried to do this to a white employee they would beat your ass and you would deserve it."

Once faced with his own racism, this man tried his best to, not defend his actions, but convince Angie he wasn't racist. Here are some of the reasons he stated. Although they are funny, these are real:

"I don't treat Benhi differently! I used to go to a Black church!"
"I have Black friends!"
"I care about civil rights!"

THE STORY ANGIE INSISTS I PUT IN THE BOOK

Angie is at that horrible church in Ohio. Even though she knows it's gonna be bad, she needs this job in Ohio to work. She goes to the meet and greet. She sees an old guy with a walker. She is avoiding him at all costs because he is old and white. She thinks he's gonna say something horrible. Even though she tried to avoid him all night, he ended up catching up with her. He was gonna say something completely nuts, and she's gonna have to quit after yelling at him. She braced for impact. He comes up to her and says, "Pastor Khabeb, I'm so glad to have you here. We are honored to have you here." I think Angie didn't want it to seem like she only had mean congregants. So, to show her you understand, please tweet at her, "Not all congregants." Just kidding, don't do that. Tweet at her, "Thank you for seeing the good in people." But spell it "peeple."

WORST NURSING HOME EXPERIENCE

Angie was visiting a church member at a nursing home in Ohio. They met in the dining area. They sat one table away from another nursing home resident who was 100 percent sure that Angie worked there. He kept asking her for his lunch and for some water. This woman was wearing a clergy shirt, and I guess this man thought, *Strange. The employees are dressing like pastors today. Good for them. Anyway, I'm hungry.* Angie tried to politely tell the old man she was a pastor. Finally, one of the staff members intervened and helped Old Man Bob back off.

MOST HOOTIE

A million years ago, Angie lived in Denver for a hot minute. When she was there, she used public transportation. On the way to work one night, a stranger at the bus stop walked right up to her. He looked so happy and so regular, she was really interested in what he had to say. What was it gonna be? Jehovah's Witness? Mormon? Does he think she's a Black person he saw on TV? He says, "Hey, I got that Hootie & the Blowfish album!" This is before Angie had ever heard of them. She had no clue what this man was talking about. But he seemed so proud of himself, so Angie tried to return the same energy, "Oh! That's great! Do you like it?" "I've been playing it nonstop!" All the while she's thinking to herself, "That's odd." Then, when her bus came a different person said the exact same thing! Now, she can piece it together. *Hmmmm, she thinks, Hootie must be Black.* Then she got to her actual job and this super jerky white guy who rarely acknowledges her presence says, you guessed it, "Hey, I got that Hootie & the Blowfish album." So strong was Darius Rucker's hold on white people that he made them feel like it was okay to walk up to Black people who were complete strangers and talk about him. *I,* he thought, *will heal the rifts racism has caused.* Bless him.

Sidenote: That was the same jerky guy who one day played the song "Baby Got Back" at work. Angie was both the only Black person and only woman present. She was extremely uncomfortable. Go ahead and come to conclusions about how they acted as that song was playing. A gaggle of white men arrhythmically humping, striking "Black" poses,

> referring to Angie and her big butt. It was bad.
> Angie complained to management, and they
> said she was "too sensitive."

Wait. Each one of us has a song, I'm just realizing! Here's Angie's! This is the song she sings whenever it's her birthday!

♪♪I'm twenty-two 'cause it's my birthday
I'm twenty-two 'cause I was born on this day
I'm twenty-two 'cause it's my birthday,
9/21/71♪♪

I feel bad for people who don't have the audible version 'cause they don't get to have these great songs.

The word "great" is doing a lot of work in that sentence.

MOST RACIST PENNY-PINCHER

Angie's husband, Benhi, used to live in Kenosha, Wisconsin, where Angie attended Carthage College, a private liberal arts college associated with the Lutheran Church. This was in the early 2000s and Benhi and Angie had recently moved to the US from Namibia. He was still growing accustomed to life in the US and this was a learning experience for both of them. They were a good ten years older than most of the students, and let's just say that Omaha, Nebraska, is like Harlem compared to Kenosha, much less that college campus. Benhi had lived through the brutal apartheid system and was quickly learning how we do racism in the land of the free and the home of the brave.

Any well-traveled person knows that when in doubt, best practice is to simply observe the locals and do likewise. One day, Benhi was in the campus bookstore to purchase a bottle of water. It was $1.04 with tax. It just so happened that a young white female student was in line ahead of him also purchasing a bottle of water, let's call her Daphne. When Daphne reaches the cash register, she already has a dollar bill in her hand. After realizing she needs four more cents to complete her purchase, Daphne reaches into her purse to find loose change. The clerk smiles and says, "Don't worry." Then she reaches into the little if-you-need-a-penny-take-one-if-you-have-a-penny-leave-one containers and removed 4 pennies and proceeded to thank Daphne for her purchase.

> Oh my god, Angie. She wrote that, but it's called "take-a-penny-leave-a-penny." What in the world has happened to your brain?

Oh no. Angie thinks she's right.

> Dear Lord. Lacey? What do you call that?

I think it's "Peter-Piper-picked-a-peck-of-pickled-pennies."

After witnessing this exchange, Benhi puts away one of the two dollar bills in his hand. The cashier rings up the purchase. "That'll be $1.04." Benhi hands her the dollar and reaches for the penny container. The cashier places her hand over the container and says, "These are for members of our community." Without missing a beat, Benhi gives her another dollar. The clerk gives him 96 cents in return. Benhi slides a quarter across the counter and asks the cashier, "May I have twenty-five pennies, please." The woman obliges and counts out twenty-five pennies. Benhi takes the twenty-five pennies and puts them in the sacred, community-only leave-a-penny container. Embarrassed, she stammers out, "B-b-b-u-t-t, I-I-I I didn't mean anything." Calmly and with a smile, Benhi told her, "That's for the next time I come in here."

MOST RACIST JOKE

While on internship in a small Lutheran church in Omaha, Angie taught a confirmation class. One of the confirmands, let's call her Heather, appeared to be very eager to see her. "Vicar Angie, Vicar Angie! I've got this funny joke to tell you." Angie loves jokes. The cornier the better. But what this junior high school student said next, really caught her off guard. Heather continued, "Now don't take this as racist or anything..." So, right there, you know a few things. This child *knows* she's wrong, and this is gonna be a joke that was racist against Black people. You also know something special: This young white child is gonna tell a Black pastor a racist joke in church, so it very well may be the worst joke you've ever heard. As she combed her mental Rolodex of what to do, she left an opening large enough for the joke to slip right in. Before she can open her mouth to stop her, Heather continued, "What do you say when you see your TV floating in the dark? Nigger, put down my TV!" Stunned yet trying to formulate a pastoral response to a child, she said, "Heather, we do not use that word. It is hurtful and represents centuries of hate." She rolled her eyes and asked, "Don't you get it? He's so black you can't see him in the dark!" Heather continued laughing. Angie thinks to herself, "Dear God, I just walked in the door!" Heaven opens up and accepts Angie. She insists on staying here a bit longer.

MOST RACIST FUNERAL

Angie served a rural church in Ohio. A retired pastor in town—let's call him Pastor Sweetheart—made sure that she had his contact information. They met for coffee, had lunch occasionally, and spoke on the phone often. He was an older pastor who wanted to take Angie under his proverbial wing.

Sadly, his health began to fail and death was imminent. Naturally, Angie wanted to attend his funeral. His service was at a congregation where she had never been before. It was a fairly large building, and she was unsure where to go. As she entered, there was a man who seemed to be loitering. He wasn't there for the funeral. Maybe he was a member of this congregation?

He doesn't come right out and ask Angie why her Black ass is in this white church. However, his facial expression, body language, and death stare made his objection to her presence abundantly clear. When pastors attend funerals of other pastors, they are invited to vest, meaning pastors are invited to wear liturgical vestments, robes, clergy shirts, or anything that identifies one as a member of the cloth.

When he notices that she is carrying her alb (pastor's robe), he thinks he's figured out her raison d'être. This idiot says in a very loud voice, "Oh, it must be time to get the robes cleaned?" Angie was pretty mad. Can she just bury one of the few people in this town that treated her like an actual human being without having to suffer through this fool's stereotypes and insecurities? She just looked at him and responded, "I'm a pastor!!" He whined, "Well, I didn't know." Resisting the strong urge to cuss him out, Angie simply responded, "Clearly."

LEAST RACIST OLD WHITE LADY

Years ago, Angie had a fantastic encounter with world-renowned educator Jane Elliott, creator of the "Blue Eyes, Brown Eyes" exercise. She was the keynote speaker at a national women's gathering. If you ever have the opportunity to see her in person, do it! She told a predominately white audience, "Stop telling racist jokes." You could feel the un-easiness bouncing around some very nervous white people. Mrs. Elliot continues, "Don't act like you don't tell 'em. We know you do." Oh my goodness, the handful of Black people who are there are laughing enthusiastically. "You want to hear a Black joke you can tell in polite company?" she says,

"Well here it is, Supreme Court Justice Clarence Thomas. That's it. That's the Black joke." She also shared a similar joke about Condoleezza Rice. Angie was honored to be part of the staff who joined her for lunch. She tried to thank her for her dedication to racial justice, but she wouldn't let her finish the sentence. Mrs. Elliott said, "Oh no, don't thank me. I could've quit anytime I wanted to, but you don't have that option!"

Angie asked her, "Mrs. Elliott, would you please do me a favor?"

"Sure, kiddo, whaddya need?"

"In the afternoon session, would you please tell the white people to stop touching my hair?"

"Of course, I will. Absolutely. By the way, do you know what to say the next time someone asks if they can touch your hair?" Mrs. Elliot asked.

"No, what?"

"You say, 'You mean on my head, right?'"

Angie did not see that one coming and she told her there was no way she could say that. She said, "That's right, because you can't get away with it. But as an old white woman I can. Listen, it's a vulgar question and it deserves a vulgar answer. But don't worry. I doubt they'll touch your hair for the rest of this conference after I'm done." This woman proceeded to make good on her word and those people left Angie the hell alone.

THE WINNER OF ANGIE'S MOST RACIST EXPERIENCE

Now, technically, there is no coming back to comedy after you read this so what I need you to do is, after you've read the whole book, put it down for a week, then come back and read this part. I mean it. It's a horrid story you will not be able to shake. Okay? You think you can handle it but don't. It is wildly off-genre. Just skip ahead to the picture of Fun Bunny.

In 2013, a man terrorized Angie and her family for three months. If it hadn't happened to her, she wouldn't have believed it.

At the time Angie is a Lutheran pastor in a bad small town. She and her family are among the very few Black people there. The whole time she was there she saw an adult Black woman once. She and her Namibian husband, Benhi, have three children and dreads. They are no one's favorite. Delphos's population is something like seven thousand and six thousand of them are members of the Catholic Church. Being Catholic is a big deal there. If someone married a Lutheran it was whispered about like a scandal. So, to be further marginalized, they weren't even Catholic.

At this point, they've lived in town for a little while. It's bad and they know it's bad. But they're trying to make the best of things. There's a ton of racism and I can't even get into those million little stories. There's only so many pages in a book, guys.

Angie's husband, Benhi, is a really nice, really happy guy but even he's having trouble. Here's a little bit about Benhi:

He grew up under apartheid in Namibia; is the nicest human being alive; and is appalled at how we Americans treat our elders.

Across the street from their house, there's a very old man who lives in an RV in his driveway. His house is actually really beautiful. It's a nice, big brick house. But it's full of at least fifty cats and they have taken over. Benhi takes pity on this man because he's an elder without anyone to take care of him. Now, the reason he's alone is because he is mean to people and no one can stand talking to him, but also he is alone and has no family. It's sad. Benhi helps this man whenever he needs it. Brings him food, offers to take him places, whatever this guy needs. At one point, this old man goes in to have hip replacement surgery and they send him back because he's too dirty. Have you ever heard of that? Someone being too dirty to operate on? When Benhi heard this he offered to bathe him. This is how nice Benhi is.

After Barack Obama is reelected in 2012, however, this old man just plain loses it. Benhi is pushing a stroller down the street with his two- and four-year-old children in it. All of a sudden, the mean old man drives toward them with his windows down. He is furiously screaming, "That nigger president is ruining this country and I'm going to run you motherfuckers outta town." He drives up onto the sidewalk and is headed right for Benhi and the kids.

They reported it. But, even with a witness, the police wouldn't listen.

After Angie had their third baby, she had postpartum preeclampsia. The doctors kept her in the hospital, and she almost died. She was reprimanded for not making it to the church's annual cookie day. A day where everyone gathers together to share recipes, trade cookies, and who even gives a shit and shame on these people.

Six months after taking this job, the committee members told Angie that if she were white she would have had the job immediately. But she was Black so they'd slept on it. They didn't want to hire her, but ultimately the bishop talked them into it.

In this small town, if you want to sit down to eat at a restaurant, you have two choices. Benhi took the two youngest to one of them. He is in a booth sitting across from his two- and four-year-old daughters.

A complete stranger approaches. He's a big tall white guy, wearing a volunteer firefighter T-shirt. Matt Dutch. "You know what these kids need? Some pecan pie." No child wants frigging pecan pie. He's insisting on it. Benhi is saying, "No thank you." But he's not having it. He goes on and on about how it's on him and they have to have it. It's gone on long enough that now Benhi knows something is wrong with this man and they're in danger. Then, this guy sits down with the kids, picks up the two-year-old, and tries to put her on his lap.

Now, everyone in the restaurant is looking. Benhi jumps up and snatches his daughter away from this guy. And as he does, this man reaches up to grab the child's leg.

Benhi shouts at Matt to leave. He does but it seems like he leaves more because everyone's looking at him than it's the right thing to do. They just so happen to be sitting across from a woman they know. She says, "I saw that. I'll come with you to the police station." Benhi thanks her but insists on going alone. At the police station, Benhi talks to the chief of police.

The chief of police goes on a whole spiel about how Matt is "a member of this community who fought for this country. He's a veteran who was in an accident so he doesn't think straight." The chief sees that this isn't enough to make Benhi feel safe. The chief adds, "The only person he listens to is his father. I'll talk to his father." And that's it. That's all they do. A child gets assaulted and they threaten to tell his dad? Well, Angie gets to the bottom of this. Turns out, the chief of police is best friends with the fire chief and the fire chief is Matt Dutch's father. His mother is in charge of the ambulances. The three of them run everything. Also, that "accident" he was in was when he was drunk driving an ATV and crashed it.

This happened on a Friday. On Sunday at church, Matt comes over to Benhi and Benhi says, "Get away from me. Right now. Never talk to me again." A lady overheard this and asks, "Why are you talking to Matt like that?" When Benhi tells her, she says, "That doesn't surprise me. I've heard to keep him away from children." So, best-case scenario: everyone is covering up for someone they all think should be in jail. Well, word gets out and his mom even gets on Facebook and posts about how awful people are accusing her son of being a pedophile. Not a smart move if you ask me but okay.

Shortly after all this, Angie is alone in her office at church. Matt Dutch comes in and shuts the door behind him. He threatens her and her family. He blocks the exit and screams at her. She finally pushes past him. It is nearly impossible to intimidate Angie. I have truly never seen her scared of anything. It's just not who she is. When she called to tell me about it I remember her saying, "He threatened us and he meant every word. *I* was scared. He scared *me*!"

One of their neighbors comes by and asks for Benhi. He says, "Matt Dutch is bragging about shooting you guys again. If I were you, I'd lock the doors. Especially your garage."

Angie's neighbor was a parole officer. He carried a gun and wasn't from Delphos so he had no allegiances. Angie told this man she was having problems with Matt Dutch and he was coming to her job harassing her. She asked him if Matt comes to the house, could she run to him so Matt doesn't hurt her family. "Maybe you can scare him with your gun." He said, "Just yell and I'll come. But I'm not gonna scare anybody. If I draw my weapon, I'm going to shoot to kill." She wondered how it had gotten to this point.

Benhi went to the police chief and asked for a restraining order. The chief explained, "They don't just give those out like candy." So, they drove to a nearby big town, and wouldn't you know it, there was a Black cop! Angie told him the whole story and asked, "What can we report? The intimidation, the assault, the stalking?" He said, "All of it." They had been so deep in the idiocy of this town that they'd forgotten it was illegal to treat them like that. "And because of this restraining order, they'll take away his guns." Turns out, the person in charge of taking his guns away was his father's best friend. The small-town police chief assured them that instead of confiscating his guns, Matt's father put them in a safe for him "until this is all sorted out."

When Benhi went to the courtroom for the restraining order, Matt walked in and sat right down next to Benhi and stared him down.

At one point, Angie was under such stress, she thought she was having a heart attack. She realized that if that were true, no one would save her. The heads of the police, the fire department, and the EMTs all hated her guts. She realized having a heart attack was not an option for her so she decided it was a panic attack and pulled herself together.

Finally, she was talking about her situation with another pastor. That pastor said, "Leave while you're still alive." For some reason, that was exactly what Angie needed to hear.

She left and found a new church. And she and her family are happy and healthy now but that church was a whole new kind of horrible time.

If you immediately skipped ahead, Fun Bunny says, "You did a good job skipping ahead!"

But if you kept reading all the way through, Fun Bunny says, "You fucked up, bud!"

CHAPTER ELEVEN

IT'S ME AGAIN!

A nd finally, the best part of the book, where I get to talk about myself. No, but these are some of my racist stories. Again, I live in New York City, and it's a completely different beast out here. I am spoiled beyond measure when it comes to getting to work with Black people and white people who are normal.

WORST TV EXECUTIVE

When I pitched a Christmas movie to one of the two channels that have a lot of Christmas rom-coms, hilarity ensued. Everyone in the industry knows that those two channels are pretty Republican. I honestly can't remember which one it is, it was so long ago. But this woman and I hop on a call for me to pitch her some holiday movie ideas and I can hear her Karen hairdo, but I think, *Who cares. This is entertainment. She can't possibly be so bad that her racism reaches me, here on this phone call.* And I say, "How are you?" and this woman who can hear that I'm a Black lady, starts talking shit about Maxine Waters. Can you believe it? And not like, normal shit that's policy-based, but like, how uppity she is and how she has no respect for people who are above her. HAHAHAHAHA. At that point in time, I know I'm not selling her anything. But, I also know she's going to listen to everything I have to say because that's how these things tend to go. So, I fire back, "It's always interesting how Maxine Waters can simply tell the truth and that triggers a lot of older, whiter Republicans. They cannot stand that she has the courage to tell them when they are only acting in the interests of the rich." This woman says, "Well, she does not know the facts, and it's clear she's speaking from ignorance. But let's just skip ahead to these pitches and stop talking about politics." If this woman thought she was gonna get one final dig in before we "started to work" she must not have known me. I said, "I agree. I don't need to defend a woman who is smart enough to have survived segregation to become a congresswoman. There's nothing she can't do. Including, I bet, write a good Christmas rom-com. We must have that in common 'cause wait till you hear these pitches!" and I went on to pitch three ideas she hated, and I never heard from her again.

WORST GIFTED PROGRAM

When I was in fifth or sixth grade, I was in a special class called Challenge for little smarties. Every Wednesday a few of us would leave our regular classrooms and meet up in the computer room to learn about things that (gasp) high schoolers would learn! We'd spend an hour with a special teacher who, I assume, went around from school to school teaching children about poetry and advanced vocabulary words and stuff like that.

Every year, they'd go to a thing called Future Probe. It was a regional competition for smarties where each school would send a team of their best and brightest. The kids would be given a global problem, and they'd be tasked with fixing it. They'd present their solution to the judges. They'd give a speech and there'd be a poster along with it to kind of advertise their solution. It was fun and you missed a day of school for it so, I really wanted to go. It would be an oasis of smart kids talking about nerd crap, and it was going to be heaven for me. No one was going to make fun of me or care at all how I looked. We gifted students didn't care too much about style or haircuts. We cared about what was on the inside. Your sweet, sweet brains.

So, after skipping first grade, after getting great grades, and after being in Challenge for a long time, I wasn't chosen to go to Future Probe. But you know who was?

Me, it was me, I was chosen. Oh wait, this isn't my Future Probe story.

Be quiet, Lacey! Anyway, in that class was a girl who we will call Sally. Sally was really nice. Unlike me, regular kids liked her. She was fun and athletic and looked like a cute little angel. I'd known her since before kindergarten because my mom babysat her. I loved that girl. But I thought it was odd she was in that class with us 'cause I knew exactly how she was doing in school. She was in remedial math but was somehow in the gifted program at the same time. Fine, but because my mom babysat her, I was literally there helping her learn how to read when she was in kindergarten. So, I told my mom that I wasn't chosen for Future Probe and Sally was. She did not care for this information. Now, let me own my part:

I was hating on her. I really was. She got to be in the gifted class and be a cool kid and be in remedial math. She had too many friends and her life was too easy and I did not think it was fair for her to get on the bus with all us nerds and take up our one time to shine. She could shine every day!

Now, it was the end of a school day and the Challenge teacher was waiting with me at the entryway of the school. I was waiting on Mom to pick me up and he was waiting so he and Mom could "have a chat." And, I'm not making this up. He leans down to me and says, "I don't know how to tell your mom this, but you're just not as smart as Sally." Pick your jaw up off the floor 'cause this man really said this. Now, I knew that if I had told my mom this, there would have to be a murder. I also knew that this man had no idea what was about to happen to him. My mom arrives and tells me to wait in the car. Whenever I think about my mom's moments like this with people, I imagine her just walking up to them and giving them a very stern yet I'm-disappointed-in-you look and them crumbling, crying, and apologizing. She'd then leave them in their shame, having done nothing but shine a light on the correct path.

Who knows what she said to him but before she talked

to him, our school was sending just one team and after she talked to him, we were sending two, including me!

So, we get to Future Probe and it's heaven. Everyone's nice. We all are having fun and we get to see nerds from other schools and it's soothing to the soul. We socialize, find our spots, and get ready to whoop ass. The event begins and they ask this year's big question. It's something like, "All life on Earth is in danger because the ozone layer is completely gone. How do you save humanity?" We are terrified. No one knows what to do. We look over to our school's second team and they are also terrified. We look around at other schools and they are hard at work, writing and thinking and achieving. We aren't. It's a panicky mess. Finally, one of us from the team is like, "We should move to the moon." Great. We all split up into teams and run with it. I quickly sketch up an idea for a poster. And it's gorgeous. Guys, not to sound like Ralphie when he turns in his report about why he should get a Red Ryder BB gun but, it was SUBLIME. And I'm not gonna go into detail about what it looked like—what's that? You *want* me to go into detail about it? Okay. For you, I'll do it. Instead of just drawing directly a flat poster, I made a crater-filled moon that hovered off the poster by putting folded paper between it and the poster board. Across the moon was a 3D banner that said something like "Life on the Moon" or whatever. And on the moon was the most lifelike cutout of an astronaut drawing you've ever seen. I've never been prouder in my life.

As far as I can remember, in Future Probe you get scored in two categories. One for how together your actual solution proposal was and one for your poster. The other team got nothing for either category but for our poster—we won! I make sure to let that fuck of a teacher know it was me who made the poster. I can only remember seeing his face twice. Once when he told me I wasn't as smart as Sally and once when I told him I was responsible for the only award our school received. Guys, I know I say this a lot about a lot of people but that teacher was a bitch.

WORST GREETING

Ooh! Did I ever tell you this? There are two separate times where I was refused a handshake. The first time, I was with my good friend in the receiving line after his mom's wedding. Even though their whole family was white, she insisted I stand with the family. I stood between her son and her daughter and as we all thanked people for coming, the vast majority of people refused to shake my hand. Even as we were talking about how beautiful the wedding was. No handshake. And, also, very little eye contact.

The second time was when I was like twenty or twenty-one I used to sing backup for a country singer. It lasted a summer and it was so fun and honestly I'm shocked there weren't more stories from then. I'm sure I just forgot them. But that whole band was so nice and happy and kind. Each of us had real jobs and did the gigs on the side. That made all the difference 'cause we were just happy to get to perform. Anyway, one year when we had just gotten offstage at a humongous outdoor event, we went to the food hall. As soon as we open the door, we see the band of a very famous country singer.

This man is still famous. I want to say his name so bad but I cannot. Also, it doesn't matter 'cause he wasn't there. It was his band. So, our manager opens the door and the entire band is there and he is like, "Wow, nice to see you guys again! You have to meet our band!" He introduces us all by name and we line up behind him. This band comes out and shakes everyone's hand but mine. Now, one story ago, in the wedding, I could see some of those people not understanding what was up and some people being grossed out, but this whole band would have rather died than shake my hand. Their faces looked like, *Who the fuck is this?* When they were just told, "Amber, our backup singer." But you know, you can feel this stuff. And that was one of the grossest collective vibes I have ever felt. Having said that, I'm pretty lucky to have that as my only backup singer story.

WEIRDEST EURO RACIST STUFF

Now, when I lived in Amsterdam, we traveled all over Europe and the world really. We had so much fun. European racism is different from American racism. They're more like, "This is how different ethnicities look and what they're good at" than they're like "each ethnicity is bad in this way." I mean, there's still plenty of racism but there's less of an undercurrent of *You people are taking over our country.* At least not directed at me. Anyways, it's a whole weird place that racist-wise, cannot compete with us. USA! USA! USA!

These are our finalists:

Okay, here is a story I tell all the time because it's so terrible.

A million years ago I used to work at a place called Boom Chicago in Amsterdam. If you talk to me for five minutes and I don't mention it, something's wrong. I frigging cannot stop talking about how this place was formative and great and awful and perfect. So, one night, I'm walking home from work and I have my headphones in. I always walk around with my headphones in when I'm out but they're only playing music 50 percent of the time. Lots of the time I just want to enjoy the city without someone rapping in my ear. Also, I was young and cute and if a strange guy was gonna come up to me, I wanted him to think I couldn't hear him talking about my butt or how hot I was...even though he was right! So, that night, I'm walking home from Boom Chicago and it's late. Now, you know how in America, people are kind of scared of Black people? Like, they don't know what we will do. Are we gonna rob them or yell at them? They're not sure but they may cross the street when they see us or clutch their purses or whatever. But in Amsterdam they, well, aren't like scared of us like that. But they very feel that way about Moroccan people. And I never really saw it firsthand until that night.

Oh my God, how many times do I reload this story?! I'm walking home from Boom and on my way past the Texaco, I see a young man, younger and smaller than me, propped up against the gas station wall. As I pass he yells something lewd. (Wow. So glad you were here for what has got to be my first time using the word "LEWD"?!) My headphones are on my head but no music is playing so I hear him and feel fine ignoring him. As I keep walking, I hear the sound of footsteps running up to me and, BAM! This guy kind of crashes into me with his arm around me and starts speaking gibberish.

It's unintelligible because he's all the way upside down on god knows what. Just eyes rolled back, damp, confused, and fucked the fuck up. He's also so small that I see him in this state and I think, *This poor child is in danger!* So, I push him off me and tell him to get out of here and I keep walking. He walks with me. I cross the street. He crosses the street. I cross the street back, he crosses the street back. I cuss him out, beg him to leave me alone; it has no effect on him. This guy is talking to me and while I don't know what he's saying, I guarantee it was drunk Dutch. A language I don't speak yet. He's also throwing some English in there: "Let's go home. I'm going to come home with you." I'm pretty sure he's trying to scare me. This guy is like very messed up but is just sober enough to track me and make sure we stay close. So, we are getting closer and closer to my house and I wonder what I'm going to do. He's so small, honestly I don't feel good about beating his ass, something that I could very do but it's a bad idea. Here's how I know:

> There was a guy who I used to work with who would, once a week after the show, grab my butt and laugh. Like every week! I don't like having my butt grabbed, so I'd beat his ass and he'd pop right up and walk away. Not to toot my own horn, but I don't think he shoulda been able to just pop right up after that. But my beatings had no effect on this guy. I had to go to my bosses and complain, something I never do. If I have a problem at work, you never have to worry about me snitching, I'm coming for you directly. Anyway, my bosses talked to him and then, it stopped. I then realized that the reason

this happened every week was that every week he did coke after work with his friends and that gave him the courage to grab my butt and the strength to take a beating. So, the moral of the story is, no matter the ass whoopin', you are not stronger than cocaine.

Back to the story. This man has been one inch away from me to my left since he saw me. I realize there may be nothing I can do. Just then, I see a taxi parked on the side of the road with the driver still in it and I think, *Great! This taxi guy will save me!* I run up to the taxi and I go, "Please help! This guy is following me and he won't leave me alone! Please take me home! I have money!" And the guy locks his door and shakes his head no. But he's not looking at me, he's looking at the guy who is following me. He's terrified of this guy. Folks, this man is 125 pounds soaking wet, how in the butt could anyone be scared of him?! I'm stunned. For once, I'm not the problem. This Moroccan guy is. Well, I'll be. I turn back to the drunk guy and, I shit you not, he says in perfect English, "Some guys are just assholes." And I laugh my butt off. I look up and I notice before we get to my apartment, that we are going to walk right past a police station. It's a crazy plan but what if he's drunk enough to let me walk him right up to the cops? Will I get arrested instead? Certainly possible but worth a shot. I turned to him and I go, "We are going home, right?" and he goes, "Yes. Let's go home." I keep walking another half a block to the police station and this little idiot never leaves my side. I walk right through the police station doors and yell, "Hey! This guy is following me home, and I think he's on a lot of drugs!" And the police go,

"Did he touch you?" And I say, "No...Wait! Yes! He put his arm around me!" The police say, "Okay. Where is he?" And I look to my left and for the first time in what feels like forever, he's not there. I run back outside and this idiot is propped up against the building smoking just like he was at the Texaco a few blocks back. I turn to the police and go, "He's right here." All at once, police spring into action. They guard me in a room and more police arrest this guy and take him back to a holding cell. They question me and notify me when his case comes up. This guy gets sentenced to four months in jail.

That story is not only about racism against Moroccans but kind of about internalized racism 'cause shame on me for thinking, *No one's gonna get mad at this guy. He's not going to get in trouble for harassing me.* And it was so affirming for an actual police force to take a crime committed against me seriously.

While we are talking about when I lived in Amsterdam, I gotta tell you this story about Germany. Me and my friend Patrick who I worked at Boom with got sent to some small city in Germany to do a show. We have the best time of our lives. It has nothing to do with the story, but it has to be said, the two of us are a party. I love Patrick, he's a very good person. Ooh! One time we were waiting to get on a tram. It was early, and we were just standing kind of next to each other (likely hungover) but looking at our phones. A stranger comes up and is kind of angrily flirting with me. It's very confusing and very aggro. I don't know what he's getting ready to do. Now, I'm fine 'cause I wish a motherfucker would, but this guy takes a step toward me and before I can say a word, Patrick is in this man's face screeeaming! Now, Patrick is not a small person and he hurt this guy's feelings so bad. The man, who I assume was at the tram stop 'cause he had some place to be, left. I say all that to let you know Patrick is a down-ass bitch.

So, on this train to Germany, we are giggling and gossiping and having such a good time, we aren't in a hurry to get off the train. As we pull into the station, I look out my window and see two police officers. I think nothing of the fact that they kind of walk along the side of the train to my car as the train is coming to a halt. I watch them as literally every last person gets off the train. They're just standing there, not interacting with anyone. Not even really looking at people. They're just talking to each other. I'm horrible at estimating but I'd call it a hundred people? So, after everyone else goes first, we finally pick up our bags and head out. We are dead last but there's a ton of people getting off the train. I mean, while we are at the tail end of at least like forty people. Each of them white. Each person walks past the police and they don't even bat an eye. My white coworker Patrick and I walk by them and they both stand in front of me to block my way. They make a move for the first time. They tell me they want to see my papers in German. I tell them I don't understand what they're saying. They switch to English, "Papers, please."

I don't want to talk about why it sends chills down your spine to hear cops in a German accent say, "Papers, please." But we all know why.

So, I hand them my passport and they look at the outside of it. They're stumped. "USA? America?" They look at me and ask "You are American?" And I say, "Yeah, man.

I'm from Omaha, Nebraska." I'm pretty sure they don't know what that is.

Fun fact: When you live overseas and tell people you're from Nebraska, many times they hear "Alaska," a place they have heard of, instead of "Nebraska," a place you just made up. And they want to talk to you about snow, which is something Nebraska also has a lot of. It takes you years to understand what is happening until one day, on a second date, a guy says something about seals and you figure it out.

So, this is a pretty blatant case of profiling. They've asked no one to see their papers but me. Now, I know Patrick and leaving these people unchecked is not his style. So, I keep an eye on him and he has stayed close enough not to draw attention but has backed away a suspicious amount. I chill out, thinking maybe he has drugs on him. Who knows? These two befuddled cops scratch their dumb heads at the fact that America has Black people whose jobs are so good that they have to travel for work. I want to say, *Why didn't you ask any other person for their passport? Is it because everyone was white and I'm Black?* But they'd have probably been like, "Yes, we assumed you were here illegally trafficking people and or drugs. And the term is 'colored.'" So, when they're done with me, I walk over to Patrick, and he was like, "Sorry I had to abandon you, I realized I don't have my passport." This man could have ended up in German jail but these people were after the only Black person. Ain't that about a bitch?

And, the winner is:

The Zwarte Piet Story! I have told this story one billion times. If you're my friend, you can skip ahead 'cause I guarantee you that I breathlessly shouted this story into your face one night while saying, "Can you stand it?!" Okay, here we go.

I was new to Amsterdam and definitely new to the Amsterdam holiday season. It is a really pretty place to be during the holidays. There are lights and in a lot of parts of town, they put up stands where you can get oliebollen and poffertjes, which are both fried-dough-pancakey-doughnut things that you need. It's also the season they put up ice-skating rinks around town. Like, pop-up ice-skating rinks and it's so pretty and Christmassy and fun.

So, once the holiday season begins, I start noticing that Dutch depictions of Santa have a little sidekick. A small man with red lipstick, an Afro, and gold hoop earrings. Cute, right? Well, reader, I am sad to tell you he is also in blackface. A full face of blackface. It's exactly as unbelievable as you think it is. And, you know how people here dress up as Santa? Well, people dress up as this guy and like, a lot. You never know when you're going to be walking down the street and one will pop up on you. Go ahead and google "Zwarte Piet." I'll wait.

Gross, right? Also, Zwarte Piet means Black Pete. Cool cool cool cool cool.

Well, I'm not going to get into the logic Dutch people have that made them think blackface is okay. And since then, it's become less popular than it was in 2004 when I saw Zwarte Piet for the first time. But these little fuckers are everywhere. They are ornaments for your tree, they are on packages of cookies at the grocery store, there's one of them frigging twelve feet high in the mall. You can't escape it. So, for me, it went from outrage to who-gives-a-shit pretty quick.

Now, as I'm getting used to this, I find out that there's gonna be a parade coming through the city with a lot of Zwarte Piets in it. So, we at the theater thought it would be funny if I went out there with a video and interviewed them in a silly way. I thought, *I love making fun of racist shit to its face. Sounds like fun!* But I was not prepared for what was gonna happen. It was magnificent. There is a huge parade that goes through the city that is almost exclusively Zwarte Piets. Guys. I mean it's six hundred of them. That's the number. I googled it. It's a sea of mostly teenage white children in blackface. Four hundred thousand spectators, many of them in blackface. It's a fresh hell. I'm shocked and I look around and see all of these people adoring Santa's helpers. They love him and I don't get it.

It's a really strange feeling to be deep in something that terrible and you're the only person who sees a problem. I would go back and forth between wanting to slap everyone to laughing my butt off. I spent the day in these feelings making a silly comedy video. Years later, I did a bit on *Late Night with Seth Meyers* about it. I'm glad I experienced that so early. It really taught me a lot about how not to slap children. To this day I haven't slapped a single child!

Lacey and I went on a tour of the Anne Frank House. We were the only people of color in the group. You go through the house where she stayed and realize how small it was and how scary it must have been. It's really moving. As you exit the tour you are asked to watch a short video. It shows a bunch of people being persecuted in today's time. People from every minority group. I remember there was a video of skinheads beating up a Jewish person.

209

It was severely unsettling. The video ends with something like this:

"These atrocities are still happening in the world. Do you think people have the right to treat people this way?"

They said Anne Frank's father added that just to make sure the experience hit home. And when it asks you that, you can vote. So, everyone voted, and we can all see how the votes are tallied. Guys. After we walked through the Anne Frank House, after we saw a video of groups of people being persecuted, there were three people who voted no. Me, Lacey, and our Black friend we went with. Everyone there hit yes! I was floored. Lacey got loud, and we joined right in. I remember Lacey saying "Well, we all know who voted no! Clearly only three people in this whole building have sense!" We were very loud about it. And I mean, just as loud as you would think but times two. "We just walked through the dang Anne Frank House and you all still voted yes? Shame on you!" What if we hadn't been there?! We made heavy eye contact with each person in there and gave them what for.

CHAPTER TWELVE

ALL DOGS GO TO HEAVEN

T his chapter is not about that. It's just a good movie you should watch with your children.

Guys. Before we go. I gotta get something off my chest.

Please let it be that ugly shirt.

Amber, you have got to shut up. Our family grew up in North Omaha. It's my favorite place on Earth. Amber and I were raised in North Omaha by our parents in a loving home along with our three other siblings. We were spoiled beyond belief. We had more than enough love, food, and land. We had more than an acre with a plethora of room to play and explore. My father grew every fruit tree that could grow in Nebraska, plus we had a huge vegetable and flower garden, which is why I'm the world's greatest gardener to this day. I know that every neighborhood has its issues, but I have been attacked with micro- and macroaggressions about living in North Omaha for a large part of my life. I have had uncountable racist conversations about living there and they continue to this day. And, since this is my book, I gotta talk about it. Indulge me.

When we were young, we didn't walk around the house saying, "Oh woe is me, I live in North Omaha!" "North Omaha" was a phrase we didn't even use. I actually found out I lived in North Omaha while attending a white church youth group in Bellevue and some of the kids decided to give all the Black kids there that nickname. "Hey North O!", instead of using our names. That was when I knew they saw being from North Omaha as something bad.

I was at the youth group one day and a friend's mother said she couldn't give us a ride home because she was afraid of getting shot. I was in JROTC Marksmanship training and I remember the teacher jokingly saying, "Wow, I know you shoot so well because you live in North Omaha and have had plenty of practice." I decided then I would not let anyone get away with telling me what a horrible place it was.

Now when I tell people I'm from North Omaha I usually get a horrible response. It's, "Oh that must have been rough," or "Wow, were you in a gang?" It sounds like a joke, but I've been asked if I was in a gang one million times.

Dude. It's Omaha, Nebraska. Let's just all calm tf down. I love that some idiot looked at the two of us and was like, "Anyone would have these two nerds as a part of their gang." Tell you what. If there was a gang out there reading comic books and doing science experiments, only then would we be 'bout that life.

So, I would like every person reading this book to hear this: Please don't say idiotic or negative comments like this to me or any other people living in North Omaha. North Omaha is not this small square block of poverty, desperation, and despair. There are good things happening here with good people to support it. I have been to social events and people have asked what part of the city I live in and when I say North Omaha the amount of racist, ignorant comments is mind-boggling.

I once had to announce in a meeting that our building was actually in North Omaha, because I had overheard someone saying that it wasn't. Every white director in the meeting, and might I add they were all from small towns in the Midwest, disagreed with me. Okay, this is where racism and ignorance are just plain hilarious. You're trying to tell me, a person from North Omaha whose childhood home is just down the street, that a building which is definitely in North Omaha is not? I was almost crying because I was laughing so hard. You're just going to sit here and try to rezone the city? Do you think you're that powerful? You're not. They were so upset that they had to say they worked in North Omaha that they all decided that they didn't. That's not how things work, you can't just decide you don't work in a certain part of the city by majority vote.

I'm currently looking for a new home and it's hilarious how many people suggest that I move out of my neighborhood because it would be "nicer." I've been told I should not invest in or start a business in North Omaha because it won't succeed. It needs to be in a whiter area. Listen, if you say these things to me I will remember them forever and file you in my brain under, "Leave This Person Alone." And let me tell you there have been a whole lot of people who have gone in that file. I'm not against starting businesses outside of North Omaha and who knows I just might one day, but what I am against is someone suggesting I do so simply for the fact that it is better where there are more white people. Do you hear how you sound? Do you know who you are talking to? I'm not that person, I'm here to support North Omaha and Black businesses ALL DAY LONG. Just like the wonderful ones mentioned here:

House of Afros, Capes & Curls; EPIC! For Girls; I AM Dance; Emerging Ladies Academy; Blair Freeman; Gamble Tech Firm; Afielda, an amazing African fashion designer; Quilterpreneur, Celeste Butler; and the reason why I'm a thousand times more beautiful than Amber, SBEaesthetics. There are many more wonderful businesses out there and I'm sad I can't list them all. We're saving that for book three! I just wanted people to know our community has some amazing things going on.

I'm glad our family and people from the community got the chance to share these stories with you. No matter how you feel about them, they have happened and are happening out there to not just a small group of people in Omaha, Nebraska, but to absolutely anyone at anytime, anywhere. I personally feel that by sharing these stories we are shining a light on racism, ignorance, and just some all-around hilarious shit. Can you do us all a favor? Please hand this book to someone that needs a good laugh, a good cry, needs to feel validated, or just needs a damn racist intervention.

And that, my friends, concludes the World Record Book of Racist Stories Awards! I'm so surprised we didn't run out of trophies. In fact, we have even more to hand out, but we ran out of pages in this book. If you've made it to this point you have now been bestowed with the power to pass out your very own Racist Awards. So put on your evening dress or top hat and make your voice heard!

We leave you with a picture of five happy babies before we knew how crap the world was!

About the Authors

Amber Ruffin is the host of *The Amber Ruffin Show* on NBC's streaming service, Peacock, and a writer and cast member on NBC's *Late Night with Seth Meyers*. She also became the first Black woman to write for a late-night talk network show in American history when she joined Seth's staff in 2014, and was a writer/sometimes performer on HBO's *Black Lady Sketch Show*.

    Lacey Lamar is Amber Ruffin's big sister. After years of working for her community, she has landed in a profession where she helps immigrants find work in their new country. Living in Nebraska, Lacey loves the challenge of creating safe spaces for the celebration of nerd/African American culture.